D1531396

"As highly as I rate Jimmy as a goalkeeper, I think he's been an even better leader for the team. All the guys respect him, he doesn't shy away from difficult situations, and he's a real connector of people. Instead of excluding guys, he brings everybody together and makes sure they all feel involved in the group.

"There are certain qualities that you look for in a player. You ask, 'Can he play the game? Does he have a good character? Is he personable? Is he marketable?' To get a full package like you get from Jimmy is rare. It's a benefit on all levels to the club, the organization, the community, the city and the team to have a guy like that on your roster."

—Peter Vermes, **SPORTING KANSAS CITY MANAGER**

"Obviously Jimmy Nielsen is a phenomenal goalkeeper, but it's the person he is outside of the white lines that makes him the ultimate fan-favorite. He's not afraid to speak of his past and share how those lessons shaped him into the person he is. His humor, winning drive and charisma demonstrate his world-class leadership for our team and our community."

—Mike Illig, **SPORTING CLUB OWNER**

"Jimmy just jumped right in, engaging with the fan base from day one. I find him to be an incredibly sincere person. I never feel like he's big-timing you. He's a gentleman who's played at the highest levels in the world and is still more than willing to just talk. He's really interested in what you have to say as a fan, and you don't find that very often in players of any sport. He also buys us beer …"

—Sean Dane, **KANSAS CITY CAULDRON MEMBER**

"The White Puma has been the cornerstone of the team. His on-the-field play has earned him recognition as one the league's best keepers. The leadership and supporter engagement has solidified his spot as a favorite within the city. We're fortunate to have him on the team and in the community."

—Clay Patterson, **SPORTING CLUB OWNER**

"I am extremely proud to be his wife, but I can't pretend it's always been easy. As Jimmy explains in this book, his gambling continued to get a lot worse in the first few years after we got married. Every time he told me he was going to quit, I believed him, because it always felt like we had such a great relationship when he wasn't placing bets. Everything was perfect when we were together, but when he was gambling, he forgot that anything else even existed. He would miss family birthdays, parties, everything, because he lost track of time.

"But I always believed that if we worked together, he could get out of it, whereas if I left, he would have no chance. There would be no reason to stop. What do you do in that situation? He was still the big love of my life, the one that I recognized as soon as I first saw him at the age of thirteen. What do I love about Jimmy? Oh boy, do you have all day?"

—Jannie Nielsen, **JIMMY'S WIFE**

"He genuinely cares about everybody. He is easy to talk to and he is always there when you need him. He's been around and he has a lot of stories. He leads by example and treats everyone equally."

—Teal Bunbury, **SPORTING KANSAS CITY FORWARD**

"All captains are leaders on the field, in the clubhouse and with management. The quest to bring championships and glory to a club is a journey that may take, in many cases, years to complete. A good captain is a leader on that journey, and a great one doesn't mind the scars that are accumulated along the way. Jimmy Nielsen is my captain, but I'm far more fortunate to call him my friend." —*Robb Heineman*, **SPORTING CLUB CEO/OWNER**

"Jimmy is an outstanding goalkeeper, and we are very fortunate to have him on our club. But more than being a good goalkeeper, he is an excellent leader, captain and person. He is great for our team and the community. Every time he speaks and represents our organization, we feel fortunate to have him here." —*Kerry Zavagnin*, **SPORTING KANSAS CITY ASSISTANT COACH**

"Jimmy is the epitome of an all-around athlete. First, he seems to know where the ball is headed before the player making the kick does, which means he's done his hard work and has a true natural gift. Secondly, our children are in the same class, which gives us a unique look into each other's lives. Jimmy's dedicated relationship with his family and our school community reflects the same energy and strong commitment that he shows on the field. Jimmy and his family are fast becoming a Kansas City treasure." —*Greg Maday*, **SPORTING CLUB OWNER**

"He's a great guy, father and husband. He has been great for this organization. The fans love him, the players love him, and he is an amazing presence in the locker room. He is very easy to work with. I couldn't ask for more from a goalkeeper." —*John Pascarella*, **SPORTING KANSAS CITY GOALKEEPER COACH**

"Jimmy is a great player and an even better person. He is a great captain who cares about his team more than anything. He is a great leader on and off the field. There couldn't be a better guy back there between the pipes." —*Graham Zusi*, **SPORTING KANSAS CITY MIDFIELDER**

"Jimmy Nielsen, with his entrancing light hair and signature bear hugs, embodies all the qualities that would go into creating the quintessential professional athlete and off-the-field personality: interesting, competitive, friendly, unselfish and genuine. Quick to stop shots while plying his trade, but even quicker to smile, the 'White Puma' has become a fan-favorite in Kansas City, while setting Major League Soccer records in the process. People watch him on the field and recognize a great goalkeeper, but he truly makes his mark on the type of man he is to every single person he encounters." —*Rob Thomson*, **SPORTING CLUB EXECUTIVE VICE PRESIDENT OF COMMUNICATIONS/DIGITAL**

"Jimmy Nielsen is the perfect ambassador for the club: personable, professional and downright good at what he does. His actions often speak louder than words. The 2012 MLS Goalkeeper of the Year still makes time for anyone. He truly is someone who everyone, young and old, should look up to, and we are so lucky to have the White Puma as our captain." —*The Curran Family*, **SPORTING CLUB OWNERS**

Special thanks to:

Photo courtesy of Gary Rohman

WELCOME TO THE BLUE ~~HELL~~ *Heaven*

Don't Bet Against the Goalkeeper

JIMMY NIELSEN
WITH PAOLO BANDINI

Requests for permission should be addressed to: Ascend Books, LLC, Attn: Rights and Permissions
Department, 12710 Pflumm Road, Suite 200, Olathe, Ks. 66062

10 9 8 7 6 5 4 3 2 1

ISBN: print book 978-0-9856314-8-2
ISBN: e-book 978-0-9856314-9-9
Library of Congress Cataloging-in-Publications Data Available Upon Request

Publisher: Bob Snodgrass
Publication Coordinator: Beth Brown
Sales and Marketing: Lenny Cohen
Dust Jacket and Book Design: Rob Peters

All photos courtesy of Jimmy Nielsen unless otherwise indicated.

Every reasonable attempt has been made to determine the ownership of copyright.
Please notify the publisher of any erroneous credits or omissions, and corrections will be made to
subsequent editions/future printings.

The goal of Ascend Books is to publish quality works. With that goal in mind, we are proud to offer
this book to our readers. Please note however, that the story, the experiences and the words are those
of the authors alone.

Printed in the United States of America

www.ascendbooks.com

CONTENTS

DEDICATION

This book is for my wife Jannie, our wonderful daughters Mille and Isabella, and also for all of the wonderful friends we have made in Kansas City. Thank you for making us feel so very much at home.

FOREWORD

Jimmy Nielsen is my captain; a simple word but with a layered narrative that is anything but simple. What does it mean to captain Sporting Kansas City? Surprisingly, the official FIFA Laws of the Game are virtually silent on the role of the captain. They pragmatically state that the captain has "a degree of responsibility for the behaviour of his team." The degree depends on the man, of course. All captains are leaders – on the field, in the clubhouse and with management. The quest to bring championships and glory to a club is a journey that may take, in many cases, years to complete. A good captain is a leader on that journey, and a great one doesn't mind the scars that are accumulated along the way.

Years ago, lying in the morning grass in Aalborg, warming up for another training session and perhaps reflecting on his career as a top-flight Danish League goalkeeper, I'm sure Jimmy never expected the twists and turns that he was about to experience in the next leg of his career journey. But for better or worse, it has been these spirals along the journey that have made Jimmy into what he is today: a brilliant, gentle giant, a family man with arms and legs of rubber that have broken the hearts of so many foes, and given rise to cheers for even more.

When Jimmy arrived in Kansas City on a February winter's day in 2010, he replaced a fan-favorite goalkeeper, and we were playing our home matches in a minor league baseball stadium. Yet not once did I hear anything from Jimmy other than appreciativeness for the opportunity to be a part of our club. Jimmy helped lead a movement to make Kansas City, previously a destination which international players were never interested in, the place to play in Major League Soccer.

In three seasons with Sporting Kansas City, Jimmy has electrified Sporting Park – diving-saves, kick-saves, double-saves, we've seen it all. They've tried everything to beat him, even an ill-conceived bobblehead toss that hit him in the eye couldn't keep him down. Jimmy helped us #PaintTheWall, and more silverware seems inevitable with him in the net. Jimmy has been everything we could have asked for in a netminder and a captain, and he surprised us with even more. Maybe the biggest and most pleasant surprise has been Jimmy's focus on winning above personal statistics. Despite the fact that Jimmy consistently ranks near the top of the League in all meaningful statistical categories, such as goals against average, saves and shutouts, Jimmy remains sharply focused on only one statistic: wins.

Save upon save. Win upon win. And yet, it's not just the moments with all eyes upon him that make Jimmy special. It's the quieter moments that happen with no one around that are the true measure of the man, like when Jimmy stops in a park to teach kids so they can one day be captains, too. It's strolling through the Country Club Plaza with family in hand, not like the modern day superhero he is, just simply a man. It's staying after practice for an hour just so kids can take penalty shots on a real professional soccer icon – and diving for each one and juuuust missing. For a person from such a foreign land, he's become our native son, and the city, the club and his teammates love him for it.

Jimmy Nielsen is my captain, but I'm far more fortunate to call him my friend.

Robb Heineman
CEO, Sporting Club

1

THE WORLD'S MOST EXPENSIVE GERBIL

"*If* they kill that gerbil, I'm going to throw a bomb in the airport."

In the long list of ridiculous things I've said throughout the years, that sentence might just be the most absurd. For starters, I don't know how to make a bomb. More importantly, I had no intention of blowing up an airport. In fact, I was well aware it's the sort of thing you shouldn't even joke about.

But those were the exact words I told our team administrator, Rick Dressel, when he pulled me aside in the middle of a Kansas City Wizards (as the team was then known) practice session in March 2010. I had only been with the club for a little over a month, and things were going great. I loved my new teammates. My family had recently flown out to join me in the US, and life was feeling pretty perfect. Or at least it had been until Rick informed me that the staff at the Atlanta airport was about to murder my daughter's gerbil.

This was no ordinary pet. Otto was, without doubt, the most expensive gerbil ever to have lived. We didn't know it when we bought him. Back then, Otto cost the same as any other gerbil, about $50 when you include the cage, the water bottle and all the other basic supplies. But getting him to America? That took thousands of dollars.

It all began when I told my family that I had received a contract offer from Kansas City. I had been playing for a team in my native Denmark, and it would mean a big upheaval for my wife and two little girls if I were to accept. I gathered them around and explained the situation. Everyone seemed excited, but my eldest daughter, Mille, had one concern. She was only willing to go if Otto could come with us.

"Of course he can," I replied. "No problem."

13

But it turned out to be a really big problem. Getting Otto to America had taken up more time and energy than I could ever have imagined. We had filled in countless forms and paid so many fees. We took Otto to the vet over and over again just so he could pick him up, look at him for five seconds and sign another sheet of paper. We had to book special animal airplane tickets, which cost more than you would pay for a human. In total, we spent more than $3,000, and my wife Jannie's parents wound up paying a couple more bills for us after we'd left Denmark, too.

And now, after all that, the authorities at the Atlanta airport wanted to kill Otto because they couldn't find his paperwork. Rick had been speaking to them on my behalf while I was out at practice, but they had told him that they were going to put the gerbil down unless they received the relevant forms within the next hour.

I couldn't get out of practice, so I had to send Rick to talk to them again. I told him to repeat exactly what I had said about the bomb in the airport, but I'm sure he was clever enough not to. Either way, he managed to persuade them to wait a little while longer. When the session was over, I came inside and started making phone calls. I got my wife, Jannie, to call her mom, since she was the one we had left in charge of getting Otto on the plane.

It turned out the paperwork had been taped to the bottom of the cage; the authorities in Atlanta hadn't thought to look. Because of the delay, Otto had now missed his connecting flight, so we had to pay another $200 for him to stay overnight with a vet in Atlanta. Two hundred bucks! You can stay in a five-star hotel for that kind of money.

Still, Otto made it out to Kansas City in the end, and Mille was so happy, it made the whole thing worthwhile. Otto was already two years old by this point, and most gerbils don't live much past that age, but he carried on to the age of five. We didn't replace him after that. My family loves animals – we have two cats and a dog at home – but I can promise you that we will never get another gerbil. Rest in peace, little Otto.

As expensive as he was, it's also true that I've wasted far greater sums of money in much more regrettable ways. As a recovered gambling addict, I know all about bad financial decisions. There have been times in my life when I lost more than $100,000 on bets in a single afternoon. Where bringing Otto to America delighted my family, gambling nearly destroyed it.

It was only by giving up gambling completely that I was able to save my marriage. And it was only by relocating my family from Denmark to Kansas City that I was able to save my soccer career.

Here he is: the world's most expensive gerbil. It cost us thousands of dollars to transport Otto from Denmark to Kansas City, but you can see how delighted my daughter Mille was on the day he arrived. Otto had two happy years with us in the States, and it was a very sad night for all of us when he finally passed away. That little gerbil was a part of our family.

2
A CHILDHOOD OBSESSION

When I was ten years old, we had a lesson at school where our teacher, Ms. Else, asked us each to come to the front of the class and write on the board the top three jobs we wanted to do when we grew up. Some of the kids had no idea at that age, but I didn't need to consider my choices for even a second:

1) Soccer player
2) Soccer player
3) Soccer player

Ms. Else was not impressed. She had been my main teacher right through from kindergarten, and she was this tough little lady in her 50s – always very fair, but not someone you wanted to get on the wrong side of. I refused to put down any other jobs because I knew that being a soccer player was what I wanted to do. She got so angry that she called my parents down to the school, where they were given this big talk about how they had to help me get my priorities in order.

"He has to focus on school now," she said. "What are the chances that he can really go on to become a professional soccer player? Physically he is here in the classroom, but his mind is always elsewhere, always dreaming about soccer. Look at his notes! There is nothing on them except drawings of soccer games."

She was right about my schoolwork, even if she was wrong to doubt my career choice. I was not a difficult kid to have in the class – I didn't scream or shout and disrupt the lessons – and I always suspected that Ms. Else quite liked me because I was well-behaved and friendly. But I didn't pay attention to what she was teaching us. Instead I would sit quietly, drawing out different formations and coming up with tactics for the teams I played for.

I thought a lot about the strategic side of the game, and when we got out onto the fields I would always be bossing the other kids around, telling them where to go and what to do. I was obsessed with soccer, but I was also obsessed with winning. I've always hated losing, be it soccer, cards, or anything else.

People ask me sometimes where I think that comes from, but honestly I have no idea. My father was a big soccer fan, but he never really played any sport to a high level. Mom had no interest in sports, and my parents used to have big arguments over how much I played. They had one that night after we came home from Ms. Else's classroom. My mom was telling him how worried she was, but my dad was just there going "uh-huh, uh-huh," not really listening. That made her even angrier.

My parents were, and still are, completely different people. I always say that my dad is the oldest teenager in the world, because he acts like a big kid. He is in his 50s now, but every Friday he goes and gets his haircut, dresses up in his new clothes – trying to look sharp – and can spend all day hanging out with people. He is a very funny guy, always cracking jokes, always the life of the party, and he just knows how to get on with people, young or old.

He is also very loud. I had one brother, Johnny, who was five years younger than me, as well as a step-sister, Heidi, who was five years older, though she did not live with us growing up. In the morning, it was normally my mom who came to wake me and my brother up, but if she was out, then my dad, instead of coming to our rooms, would shout from the kitchen of our apartment:

"JIMMY! JOHNNY! IT'S TIME TO GET UP!"

I used to lie there thinking: *Oh, no,* but he would keep on going, so loud that the whole building could probably hear him.

"COME ON! COME ON! WAKE UP!"

"I am awake."

"I DON'T SEE YOU! GET UP! GET UP! GET UP!"

My mom is the complete opposite of my dad in almost every way. She's small, she's quiet, and she rarely shouts. Maybe once in a whole

18

year she might lose her temper and shout a little bit, and when she does, you listen. I suppose they both shared an interest in fashion, and she was always very well dressed.

But as unusual as it sounds, the family member I played soccer with the most when I was little was my grandmother. My parents owned a few bars and nightclubs together – that was what they did for a living – so if they were out at night managing those, I would usually get left with my granny, who lived in another apartment right across the street. I spent a lot of time with her growing up, to the point that she was like a second mom to me. I have nothing but good memories of the time I used to spend with her. We were so close that, when I first started playing soccer at around three years old, I only wanted to do it if she could join in as well. She needed crutches to get around at that time, so rather than play outfield, she would go in goal. She used the crutches to her advantage, lifting them up and knocking away shots with them.

I remember very vividly the time when I accidentally hit her in the face with the ball. It was just us two that day, with me taking shots and

I was lucky that I always got along with my two siblings. My brother Johnny was a professional soccer player himself but was forced to retire early due to knee injuries. My stepsister Heidi is a psychiatrist. She definitely paid more attention at school than I ever did.

her trying to save them with those crutches. She didn't normally wear her reading glasses when she went out, but for some reason she did that day, and the ball smashed them right up into her face. She got this big cut just above her eye, right in the corner next to her nose. The glasses were completely broken, too. She was bleeding quite badly, but our plan had been to go play a little soccer and then get an ice cream, and she still took me for the ice cream. She was holding a piece of paper up against the cut with one hand and eating her ice cream with the other. That's what she was like: a tough lady who wouldn't even have thought about rushing off to the hospital or anything like that. And she never let that incident put her off from playing soccer again. The next time I asked, she was back in goal and stopping shots with those crutches.

As I got older, of course, I played less with my granny and more with my peers. At four years old, I joined the kids' team of the local professional club: Aalborg BK. It's a gigantic club – the biggest for 100 miles in any direction – and they have a huge youth setup, with an Under-5 team, an Under-6 team, an Under-7 team and all the way up to the Under-21s. European soccer clubs like to get hold of kids young, before anybody else has a chance to spot the talented ones!

Everyone in our city supported Aalborg. It's funny to think about it now because, to me, Aalborg is not a tiny city – in fact, it is the fourth-biggest in Denmark – but the whole country is on a completely different scale than the United States, and more people live in the state of Missouri than in the whole of Denmark. I think the population of Aalborg is about 175,000 if you count all the suburbs around the main city.

But perhaps because Aalborg is that size, it is also one of those places where the soccer team really means everything. Denmark is not like the United States, where you have lots of different sports like football, baseball and basketball competing for people's attention. Soccer is the No. 1 sport by a long way, and you can feel the whole mood of the city lift when Aalborg is winning. But when it's losing, you can walk around town all day and not see anybody smile.

I would eventually grow up to be their starting goalkeeper, but back then I was playing outfield, and my career was nearly ended before it had even begun. I was still just four or five, and I don't even really remember what happened, but I was playing in a game one day when suddenly I took a ball really hard to the face. Unlike my grandmother, I did not soldier on. In fact, I decided then and there that I did not want to play soccer ever again.

Just like that, I quit playing for the Aalborg Under-5 team. But, of course, I was still fascinated with soccer, so I would still watch games on TV and play on my own in my room at home, kicking a ball against the wall or whatever.

Then, about a year later, I started school. All my friends there were playing for the same youth soccer team, B52, and they started asking me to come down and join in. I thought about this a little bit and said, "I will only play if I am allowed to go in goal."

Somewhere along the line I had come to the conclusion that if I could protect my face with my hands, I would never again get hit by the ball like I did on that day with Aalborg. I should have known better from what had happened to my granny at the park, but I suppose I just thought that she couldn't protect her face because of the crutches.

The first team I ever played for was the Under-5 side of our local professional soccer club, Aalborg. I didn't always play in goal back then, but I guess I did on this particular day, because I've got the gloves on.

21

Of course, the reality is that goalkeepers get the ball kicked at their face more than any other position, but at five or six years old, I hadn't worked that out yet. If I had, then that probably would have been the end of my soccer career right there and then!

In any case, my friends were very happy. They didn't have a goalie at that time, so straight away I became the starter. I was pretty tall already, which helped a lot at that age, and from that day on I have always been in goal – whenever I was playing seriously, anyway. As I got older, I would gradually start playing outfield again in casual pick-up games with my friends.

I have to say, though, I had an awesome childhood. The neighborhood where we grew up – Gug, a suburb of Aalborg – was so safe, and it was mostly families with kids, so I had lots of friends nearby. We had this huge park where we could go and play soccer, and it was close enough that we could just get a few guys together and walk over there. Very soon it was where I would spend all of my free time.

My friends and I would be out there every day – we didn't care if it was sunny, raining or snowing. There were a few kids who would always go down there with me, including my best buddy, Mikkel. He was not quite as crazy as I was about soccer because he wanted to grow up to be a teacher. His parents are teachers, his aunts and uncles are teachers, everybody in his family is a teacher. Now he is a teacher, and his wife is a teacher, too. Now that I think about it, I suppose it's quite funny that my best friend should be a teacher, given how little I used to care about school!

But Mikkel lived right across the street, and even if he wasn't quite as obsessed with soccer as me, he was still always ready to play. We would head out to the park and have these ridiculous, epic games that went on and on. We would play anybody who wanted to have a game against us, which sometimes meant that we would be up against a team of much older boys. I loved that. You should always want to play against people who are better than you, because that is how you improve and learn new things.

Since I hated losing so much, we always had to keep playing for one more goal and until my team had the lead, no matter who we were up against. Sometimes that meant carrying on even after it got so dark that you could barely see the ball and their players had started to quit and head home. We just kept going and going. Then finally we would score to take the lead, I would whistle and that was it, full-time. I never lost in those games.

Looking back now, it is a little crazy how long we spent out there on that field. There were no adults looking after us: we just played on our own until well after dark. I would not let my kids do the same thing nowadays because it is just not safe. The world has changed, sadly, and I feel very lucky to have grown up in a time and place where it was possible to be like that and not have to worry about it.

That said, even if things had been different when I was younger, I'm certain I would have found ways to play. As it was, I would soon start skipping school so that I could practice even more than I was already. When you have something inside you like I had with soccer, you cannot keep it shut away.

Howdy partner! This is one of the earliest pictures I have of my childhood, and for some reason, I'm dressed as a cowboy. We don't really celebrate Halloween in Denmark, so I must have just liked that outfit.

3
LESSONS IN GAMBLING

Just like the soccer, my gambling started young. Once again, my granny was involved. Whenever we were not at the park together, we would sit in her little apartment, playing cards and drinking coffee. She loved her coffee, and I learned to love it too, as I sat opposite her at the table. It was always the same game – Rummy – and she would always have us play for a little bit of money. Not big bucks, maybe only a quarter for each game, but we could play for hours.

That must have started when I was about five years old, and it carried on all the way through my childhood. When dad was around, he would play with us. Granny was his mother, so I guess they used to play together when he was little. By the age of seven or eight, I would

This is me with my granny, sitting on the couch at my parents' old house in Aalborg. I loved hanging out with her as a kid, so I have no idea why I'm looking so unhappy in this photo.

be the dealer, and I could cut and shuffle those cards like a pro. They should have had me working in the casino!

I suppose gambling ran in the blood. My father loved going to the horse races, and he used to take us all on big family outings there. Like most people, he would have a few bets at the track, and when I got to about twelve, he decided it was time for me have a go, too. He gave me 100 Danish Krone – the equivalent of about $20 – and told me the name of the horse I had to put it on.

Being a kid, I decided not to take that $20 straight to the betting kiosk but instead went to the food and drink concessions. I bought myself a hot dog, a soda, some chips, all the sort of stuff that you want when you are that age but which your parents won't always let you have. So by the time I went to put the bet on, I only had a little bit of money left.

Of course, the horse won. It was good odds, 25-1, I think, so if I had placed the full $20 on that bet, I would have made $500. I remember as it was coming home my dad was getting so excited and shouting at me, "You've won! You've won!" I didn't want to say anything because I hadn't told him about the soda and the hot dog. I still won some money, but it was nothing compared to the amount it should have been.

Years later, when my gambling started getting serious, I would do almost the exact opposite – telling my friends and family that I had only bet a small amount on a race or a game when actually I had thousands of dollars riding on it. I got very good at hiding the extent of my wins and losses. But back then, as a twelve-year-old kid, I had to tell my dad exactly what had happened because he wanted to know what I was going to do with all that money.

Still, from that moment on, I was hooked on the horses. I never wanted to go hug and kiss them or feed them like some other kids did, but I did think they were incredible animals. To see all those big, strong creatures coming down the track, I found that very charming. Going to the races in Denmark is not just about gambling – it's a very family-friendly environment with a playground for the kids, and people having picnics and barbeques – but placing a bet definitely made the day more exciting for me.

As you can probably tell, gambling was something my family did quite a lot together, except for my mother, who was never that keen about it. It was also something that suited my personality very well, giving me more opportunities to compete and, more importantly, to win. So after a while, I started coming up with new ways to have a bet with my friends as well.

It started with video games. Very often, during term-time, a group of us would get together right after school to play Sensible Soccer. I'm sure older readers will remember it, but it was a top-down soccer simulator that was very basic but so much fun. Five or six of us would all go to somebody's house as soon as we got out from school and would stay there for hours playing that game.

After a while, to make it even more exciting, I set myself up as the bookie. We would set up a tournament where one guy played as Ajax, one guy as Liverpool, one guy as Barcelona, and so on until we had the right number. Then I would decide the odds for each person, and they would all bet against each other on who was going to win.

To make sure nobody cheated, they could only bet on themselves, and if we were ever having a little trouble getting enough guys to take part, I would change the odds to make it more attractive to our friends who said they weren't going to play. When somebody came to me saying, "No, I can't do it today, I have to help my mom," I would make their odds 8-1 or 10-1, bigger and bigger, until they got so desperate that they found a way to get out of that commitment. You needed to have the right number of players to make it worthwhile.

That was a lot of fun. The only game I liked more than Sensible Soccer was Championship Manager, where you took charge of a team and got to sign the players and pick the tactics. The kind of stuff I was doing in school every day, when I was meant to be working! I always liked to take over a smaller team and see how many seasons it would take me to get them up to the top division.

I played that game a lot, and I do mean *a lot*. By age fifteen I had a computer in my room, and I used to sit up and play that game all night. At some point, I would look up at the clock and go: "Oh my God, it's 1:00 a.m., but I'll just finish this one game," and then the next time I looked it would be 2:30. It was ridiculously addictive.

Taking bets on video games was just the start, though, and after a while I decided that I could be the school's bookie for real games as well. There is a big English bookie called Ladbrokes, and because my father used to gamble quite regularly, I knew that they published a list every weekend with all the games on it – just one big sheet where you filled in the boxes for each game you wanted to put some money on and then sent it off to Ladbrokes to place your bet.

There is no Ladbrokes branch in Denmark, but by calling up their phone line and giving them a fake age, I was able to get them to start sending that slip to my house every week. I was only thirteen or fourteen, but I told them I was five years older.

Once I had the list, I would take it into school and show it to my friends. They could see all of the odds for the weekend and they would place their bet with me, just like an adult would with Ladbrokes. The stakes started out pretty small – maybe one or two dollars for a game – but over time they started to get a little bit bigger. Kids were bringing in their money for lunch and were spending it on placing a bet with me!

The school was huge, hundreds and hundreds of kids going from kindergarten right through to 10th grade, and very soon word got round about what I was doing. Instead of bringing in just the one list, I had to make twenty copies and then hand them out to different people who would share them around. It was not just kids from my grade but much older ones, too, who would come to me for a bet.

What I was doing was probably pretty crazy. Ladbrokes or any other bookie had a large amount of money stored away to pay people out with, but I really didn't, at least not to start off with. I guess they must have had a pretty good business model, though, because my reserves grew pretty quickly. I soon had at least a few hundred dollars together, which I kept in my locker at school.

Unfortunately, that was my big mistake. Just when it was all going really well, somebody broke into my locker and took it all. I never found out who it was, but I guess by that stage most of the school knew what I was doing, so it could have been anybody. There was nothing I could do to find out because if I told the teachers, they would have wanted to know what I had been doing taking those bets in the first place.

I cannot tell you how deflating that was. I had become so famous at the school by this time that I had at least thirty guys betting with me every week, but I stopped straight away after that. More than being angry, I just remember being really disappointed because it was something that I had enjoyed doing so much. It was fun having that extra money, and it was exciting looking out for the scores each week to find out if I had won or not.

My parents never found out what I had been up to, but not long after I shut my little business down, my father opened up his own real bookie. Like father, like son, I guess. And perhaps a little bit like grandmother, too.

4
SOCCER GETS SERIOUS

My first great save happened when I was eleven years old. I was playing for that same club team, B52, where I first decided to go in goal.
We were having a terrible season, bottom of the league. The game
was away from home against our local rival, Vejgaard, which was in
first place.

If that game had gone as it was supposed to, we would have lost
by 10 goals, but somehow we came out with our best performance

*The team I played with through most of my childhood: B52. I'm crouched down in the
front row, in the goalie's uniform. My best friend Mikkel is next to me; he's the only
one not looking at the camera! We were the first team in B52's history to play in the
top league at the Under-12 age group. I'd love to take credit for that, but actually it
was the team from the year before that got us promoted. They then moved up to the
next age category, and we replaced them in the U-12 league.*

in months, and with time running out, we were up 1-0. They were throwing players forward, with all their guys in our half trying to get the tying goal, and we were just hanging on, defending as much as we could to try to keep our lead.

Finally, with a minute left to go, one of their forwards got a little bit of room in the area and had this shot which deflected off another player on the edge of the six-yard box. I had already dived toward where the ball was originally going, so I was lying on the ground. But I managed to jump back up and get an arm out to push it away. Unfortunately, that wasn't enough. The ball fell right to another big forward who was running in at full speed. He cannot have been much more than a yard away from me and he just absolutely crushed his shot, but in that split-second, without thinking, I kicked out my leg in the direction he was shooting. The ball hit my shin and went up over the crossbar.

It was a sick save, a crazy save to be making at that age. The forward could not understand how his shot hadn't finished up in the net. As soon as the final whistle blew, our coach ran over to me and shouted, "What a save!" Then the referee came over to me and said the exact same thing. Even the opposing team's parents came over to me and said, "Wow! What a save!" I was getting so high on the adrenaline of it all.

That was the moment, right there, where I absolutely knew I was going to make it. Like I have already told you, I had decided from a very young age that I wanted to be a professional soccer player, but this was the moment when I knew that I could be a really good one.

The double saves like that are the ones I am the most proud of because you need to be so quick to make them. Before I joined Sporting Kansas City in 2010, my favorite was one I made for the Danish club Aalborg, against Aarhus. A cross came over from the right, and the forward made a diving header that was going into the bottom right corner before I threw myself down there to block it. The ball bounced out into the area where another Aarhus player headed it back toward the top left corner, and I had to spring back up and all the way across the goal to push that one away.

My best save in America was similar to the one I made for B52, and it was in a game against Seattle in 2011. Mike Fucito had this powerful shot from the edge of the box. I threw myself down to push it away, but immediately Lamar Neagle came running in toward the goal from the right-hand side. He tried to smash the ball in at the near post, and I just had time to get up, run two steps back toward him and get my leg out there for the kick save.

People ask me sometimes what goes through my head at a time like that, but the honest answer is "absolutely nothing." There is no time to think, because as soon as you start thinking, you will slow down your reactions. Like the Nike commercial says: Just Do It.

Anyway, by this stage, I was getting to be a pretty good goalie. At regular intervals each team in our age category had to put forward its two best players to represent the region, and the selectors would take sixteen players out of that group to take part in competitions against kids from other parts of Denmark. I would always get called up for those games.

I have to give my father some credit here as well, because he came up with a very clever trick to make sure I always worked hard and

From the age of about 11 or 12, I started getting called up to represent our region, Nordjyske, in games against kids from other parts of the country. I always got selected together with my B52 teammate Anders, and he's the one standing next to me in this shot. He was a very good midfielder, but at a certain age he left town and, as far as I know, he never played professionally.

stayed focused when it came to my soccer. Not that I ever stopped being obsessed with soccer, but when you get to twelve, thirteen years old, suddenly there are a few other things that start to get a little bit interesting, too – like meeting girls and going to parties.

We had a few big battles in our house about things like that. My friends would all be going to some party, but because I had a game the next day, my father would tell me that I couldn't go. And whenever I tried to argue with him, he always came back with the same answer: "OK, you can go," he would say. "You are absolutely free to do what you want, but I will tell you one thing: You cannot do it all. If you want your dream to come true, you have to take it seriously. If not, then you can always be a mailman."

Now let me say straight away that there is nothing wrong with mailmen, but the mailman in the neighborhood where we lived had the worst job in the world. It was all blocks of apartments with no elevators, so he was walking up and down those steps all day, working like a horse. Every time I saw him, he would be carrying this big heavy bag with all the mail, and sweat was just pouring off him. So, yeah, I had a pretty scary image in my head of what it would be like to have the mailman's job. Every time my dad said that, I would think: *Jesus Christ, I do not want to be that mailman.* And I would wind up staying home again.

That is not to say I never went to any parties – I still went to some – but my dad was right that you have to make sacrifices to follow your dreams. There was a youth club that my friends and I all used to go down to every Tuesday night, and I remember when I was about thirteen they organized a big skiing trip to Norway. It was only for one week and would have meant missing just one game, but my dad wouldn't let me go.

All of my friends went on that trip, and it was going to be a big chance to spend time with some of those girls I was getting interested in. I was angry, I was shouting, I was slamming doors. But in the end, I was not allowed to go. It was a funny thing with my dad that he didn't push me with my studies, only with soccer. I don't remember a single time he asked me about my homework. Not one. But at least by that age I had met some other kids who were taking soccer as seriously as I was. The only problem was that they all lived in a different country.

About a year before that missed skiing trip, I had been sitting at home after school one day when my mom called me from one of the nightclubs that she and my dad used to run. She told me she had been contacted by a guy who was in charge of a tournament taking place nearby and who wanted to know if I would be interested in playing for "that English team." Of course my mother – not caring about soccer – could not remember the name.

It didn't matter to me anyway. When had I ever turned down a game of soccer? I said that I was interested, took the number, and called the guy right back. It turned out that it was the Under-12 team of Norwich City, whose senior side at that time was playing in the top division of English soccer. Their regular goalkeeper was sick, so they needed somebody to fill in.

That was very exciting to me. English soccer was a big deal in Denmark, and they used to show a game on Danish TV every Saturday during our league's winter break. They also had a show every Wednesday where they would give you a look at the teams playing that weekend, and I watched it every time. More than anyone in Denmark, my goalkeeping hero growing up was Everton's Neville Southall, who was this big guy with a huge, black moustache and lots of personality. He had a bit of a belly, too, but that didn't stop him from being a great goalkeeper.

So off I went that weekend to play with Norwich in that tournament, and from the very first second I met their players, I knew this was something completely different from anything that I had been a part of before. They had an incredible soccer mentality; every one of them wanted to compete and to win. Right from kickoff, they were yelling at each other, giving instructions, telling each other off. I thought: *This is paradise!* I was used to playing in games where I would be the only guy on either team doing these things.

It was an amazing few days. We won the tournament, and I got an award for being the best goalkeeper. Afterward, one of the assistant coaches pulled me to one side. "Listen," he said. "We want you to come to England and play for us."

I would have said yes right there and then, but of course things were not so straightforward. At twelve, I was still far too young to be signed to a proper contract, so the only way for it to work would be for my parents to move over to England – with the club helping them to find some work nearby – or for them to sign over guardianship to another family over there.

My dad would probably have let me go from the age of three, but my mom was not going to consider anything like that. So Norwich suggested that I could just fly over on weekends to play in the games. Every Friday I would head out to the airport and catch a plane to wherever the team was playing, usually England, but sometimes different tournaments around Europe as well. They would pay for my flight over, and each time I would stay with the family of a different teammate.

Well, that was the theory anyway. There was one occasion when things really didn't work out that way.

The game that week was in England and the team had booked me a plane ticket to London's Heathrow airport. I was not even thirteen, and it was only the fifth time I had ever made the trip over to play for Norwich. I had never flown on my own before I started training with them, so to make it a little easier, Norwich would have a driver meet me at the airport when I landed, hold a sign up with my name on it and take me where I needed to go.

But this time when I came through the arrivals gate, there was nobody waiting. My first thought was that he might be late. This was in the days before mobile phones, so after having a good look to make sure I hadn't just missed him, I tried to wait. But Heathrow is not an easy place to relax. It's one of the biggest airports in the world; there are people coming and going in all directions, and to a twelve-year-old kid, it was pretty intimidating. Bear in mind that I didn't speak very good English at this point, either. That might have been the first time I ever wished I had tried a little harder in school!

Norwich required us to show up for every game and training session in a suit, which was normal enough for the English kids who all had to wear uniforms for school, but it wasn't for me. I was used to wearing jeans and a t-shirt to class. I didn't even own a suit, so my parents had taken me out to buy a few. Now I was standing in the middle of this huge airport, wearing my jacket and tie and dress pants. I looked like a big man on the outside, but I felt tiny on the inside.

I didn't have the phone number of any of the coaches or players in England. The only number I had was for Henrik, the man who organized that first tournament I played for Norwich. He acted as the team's contact in Denmark, and whenever they needed me for a game or a competition, he would be the one to call me up and check that I could make it before he booked the ticket on their behalf.

Eventually, it became clear that the driver was not going to show up. I went to find a phone box to call Henrik from, and all I can say is thank God I had a good amount of English money with me that day. International calls were a lot more expensive back then, especially from a phone box, so I just remember throwing coin after coin into that machine. Henrik picked up the phone and by the time I said "Hello," it wanted another coin. "It's me, Jimmy." Another coin. "Nobody came…" Another coin. "… to meet me." Another coin. I put so much money into that phone box, calling him over and over to try to get another update.

I hadn't flown out until Friday evening after school, so it was getting late by this point. Norwich is not even that close to London – about a three-hour drive – and I was getting pretty worried. Finally, several hours after I had landed, they worked out that nobody was coming to get me and agreed instead that I should go to a hotel. Henrik gave me the address for one near the airport and told me to get a cab down there. Remember, I was twelve.

The hotel was not like one of these big ones you have in America, or even like one of the motels you get along the Interstate. It was pretty much just somebody's home, a little townhouse with maybe three or four rooms in it. A 'bed & breakfast,' as they call it over there.

It doesn't sound like a big deal now that I am an adult, but back then, that was pretty scary stuff for me, walking into a complete stranger's house and staying the night. I had no easy way to phone my parents, and I didn't even know if anyone was going to pick me up the next day – I had just been told to go there and wait – so in the morning, I sat waiting, and waiting, and waiting. I don't know what time they finally came, but it felt like I had been there forever.

I also had no idea, while I sat there waiting, where our game was being played that day or who it was against. It turned out to be something rather special. When the driver finally came, he took me directly to Carrow Road, Norwich City's home stadium. We were playing our game out on the main pitch before the senior team had their match later in the afternoon.

It was pretty exciting to walk out onto the field of a professional English soccer club which I had watched on TV. When our game started, they had not yet opened up the gates to fans, so at the beginning it was just rows of green and yellow seats and some concrete standing areas, but as we got near to kickoff in the senior team's game, people started coming in.

When it's full, Carrow Road can hold more than 25,000 people, and though a lot of those weren't really paying attention, some of them started to cheer for us. The funny thing now is that I cannot remember who the game was against or how the score went. I just remember being very excited to be out playing in that stadium.

You can probably guess how my mom felt about me playing for Norwich, especially after I told her everything that had happened with the airport and the hotel. She didn't stop me, though. I just made sure I was always a little more organized for my trips with Norwich after that, and I always called Henrik on the day before I flew to make sure that there was going to be somebody waiting for me. It didn't happen again.

Those next few years turned out to be an amazing time for me. We played in tournaments all over Europe – Spain, Holland, Italy and France – but what really excited me was just being in that environment, working with guys like that every weekend. The coach, Kit Carson, was unbelievable. All the coaches I had in Denmark at that age had full-time jobs and only coached for fun. He was a full-time, professional coach, and he created a completely different environment.

After every game, you would go into the locker room and wait for Coach Carson to come in and put his ratings up on the board. He gave every player a number out of 10. If you got 10, then you had played an absolutely incredible game; if you got a 6.5 or 7, then you had done OK, and if you got a 3 or a 4, you had been awful.

As well as giving those scores, he would name the best three players on the team – MVP, runner-up, and third place – and also the three worst. He would write a little comment under each name, saying what the person had done well or done badly. So for that age it was pretty serious. My name was in the bottom three sometimes, which was no fun but not nearly as bad as it seemed to be for some of the other kids. They would start crying because they were so scared about having to tell their parents.

My parents were not like that. I could get into fights with my dad about soccer; that happened a lot of times, but it was never because of a bad game or a bad performance. It was always about whether I had put enough effort in and whether I was doing enough practice. He wanted me to practice all the time, and if I had to do something with friends, we would go back to that same argument. I would be there saying, "Dad, I practice all the time. This is just one day I am skipping." He would reply, "If you want to follow your dream, you cannot skip." And once again, the mailman would come up. Every time he mentioned that, I would always wind up going to practice.

Coach Carson was helping me out with the practice I did back home in Denmark, too. Every two weeks he would give me a report card grading me on each different skill that a goalkeeper needs – shot-stopping, crosses, and one-on-ones. Then, underneath the grade, he would write down some drills that I could show to my coaches back home.

The only downside of playing in such a serious football environment was that after a while, even I had some competition for my place in the team. When I was fourteen, an English goalkeeper, Mark Tyler, showed up, and he was also very good. He was a few inches shorter than me, but he had great reflexes. Not long after he arrived, we were playing in a tournament in Finland where Coach Carson decided we should alternate games. So I played one game, then Tyler played the next game, then I had the one after that, and so on.

We made the final of that tournament, and on the day of the game Norwich took us to a nice hotel – we had previously been staying somewhere a little cheaper – so that we could use the facilities there for a few hours. We took cold showers, ran into the steam room and back into the cold shower, then into the sauna. We were having a little bit of fun and relaxation before the game.

At some point we went to get lunch, and while we were eating, Coach Carson came and asked me to go have a conversation with him in the other room. When we got there, he sat me down and told me, "You have done really well in this tournament, so please don't be too disappointed, but I do have some bad news: You are not playing the final. Mark is going to start that game."

I said, "All right." He just sat there and looked at me for a second, like he was waiting for something.

"Why are you not crying?"

I said, "Am I supposed to cry now?"

"Well," he said, "every other kid I have had in here today cried when I told him he was not going to start."

"It is what it is," I said. "You have made your decision, Mark is going to start. What is the point in me crying about it?"

That was really how I felt. I probably should have been more upset about it, because Mark had played the semi-final, so if we had kept on alternating, it would have been my turn to start. But in that moment I just did not feel like crying. Again, maybe it had to do with the different pressure that those kids were under compared to me. At that age it was almost life or death for them. I wanted to play and to win – I still hated to lose – but football was still fun for me.

That said, the game itself was a little harder. It's not fun to watch a game when you could be playing. It doesn't matter what age you are, you want to be on the field, and when the game was on, that was probably the first time in my life I had felt the disappointment of not playing.

As we got older, it only got more serious. The coach would take us to watch the senior team practice at Carrow Road, and seeing that was very intoxicating. I remember coming away from one of those sessions and just thinking to myself: *This is the life I want to live. I want to play in that goal someday.* I was practicing hard every day to make sure it happened.

I still didn't feel under pressure, though. From fifteen years old, Norwich could sign you to a proper contract, so as we got toward that age, everyone else on the team was talking about that more and more and speculating about whom would get a deal. It was not on my mind at all; I just enjoyed being there every week in that environment.

On one of my last trips over to Norwich, we had to play a couple of games on the same day, and in the first one I got a really painful charley horse. I was struggling to walk, let alone make saves, but the coach came over to me between the two games to have a word.

"Jimmy, don't worry about anything. Of course you are going to get offered a contract."

"What do you mean?"

"You don't have to limp around and pretend to be hurt if you are worried about not playing well."

"But coach, I am really hurt. I can't even bend my leg."

"Don't you worry, son. You're going to be fine. You'll get that contract."

I didn't know what to say, because honestly, that hadn't been on my mind for even a split-second. He probably knew a little something about the English guys and their mentality, but maybe I was different.

Not long after that, the contract offer arrived. It was just before my fifteenth birthday, and I was in England for a weekend of practice. On that Saturday, we all got together for a big team lunch and, as I recall, we were all sitting there at this long table, with the players together in one group and the coaches a little farther down. All the players were talking about contracts. There were a lot of guys on that team, and you knew that only one or two players from each age group were going to make it. The money in England is so big that if teams don't like the players they have in their youth team, they just go buy somebody else instead.

Everybody was asking me that day when I was going to sign with the team. I know the coach had already told me I was going to get a contract offer, but I guess it still hadn't sunk in, because I wasn't sure if it was actually going to happen. I was just sitting there saying, "I don't know," trying to change the subject.

The next morning we had practice, so at that point I got up a little courage and went and spoke to the coach, saying, "Everybody is talking about contracts – am I getting one?"

He said, "Yes, we are sorting that out."

Now I really believed it. Right after practice I went to another phone box, put a bunch of coins in, and called home. My father picked up.

"Dad, they want to sign me!"

"I know, I know… relax. I have already talked to them. We are going to sort something out, so don't worry about that and just have fun."

At this point, I was walking on air. I finished practice for the weekend, got on the plane back to Aalborg, and all I could think about the whole journey was telling everybody back home. My mom was waiting for me at the airport to pick me up.

"Mom! Mom! Norwich City is going to sign me!"

"Hey, hey, hey. You better relax here. Relax. What is important right now is to concentrate on doing well in school."

"But Mom, this is …"

"We are not going to talk about that right now. We will talk about that later when your father is here."

You can probably imagine how those conversations went. My dad wanted me to go; my mom did not. They had a few really big arguments about it. The last I remember it being discussed was one night when we were driving back from seeing a few friends. We were going down the highway, and my dad was explaining again why he thought I should go. All of a sudden, my mom slammed on the brakes so hard that the car screeched to a stop right there in the middle of the road. Now she was really yelling.

"MY SON IS NOT MOVING TO ENGLAND! HE IS ONLY FIFTEEN YEARS OLD, AND HE IS STAYING RIGHT HERE TO FINISH HIS STUDIES!"

Nobody said anything after that. We were not used to hearing my mom lose her temper, and we drove the rest of the way home in silence. There were no more discussions on the matter. My parents told Norwich that I was not allowed to go, and that was the end of it. I never played for them again; at a certain point, they are not going to keep paying for you to go back and forth without having you signed to a contract.

I was disappointed because I really loved the group of guys I was playing with over there and, like I said, I didn't know anybody in Denmark who had that same appetite for soccer. I'm sure that Norwich was disappointed, too, after spending that money to fly me over. But on a personal level, I never heard anything bad from them. Coach Carson eventually moved on from Norwich, but he kept taking his teams to Denmark for tournaments, so I saw him a few times and would go and say hello. I will always thank him, because those years were an important step for me as a soccer player.

It was over now, though. It was time for the next phase of my soccer career – and, also, my gambling career.

You've seen the 'before' picture, so now here's the 'after' – me with a couple of my B52 teammates now that we're all grown up. On the right of this picture is Mikkel, who went on to become a teacher, just like he always wanted to do. On the left is Dennis, who also played with us on that team and is another of my closest friends. He works as an investor.

5
TEENAGE KICKS

Around the time I stopped playing for Norwich, my father opened up his betting shop. It was a good size, split over two floors with space for 100 people. Downstairs was the bookie, which had counters where you could place your bets and TVs up on the wall showing sports all day long. There was also a pool table right in the middle of the room, so you could hang out there even if you didn't want to gamble. Upstairs was nothing but slot machines.

There was always a great atmosphere, with people joking and chatting about soccer. Most of the time when you walked in you wouldn't even be able to see the other side of the room because the whole place was thick with cigarette smoke. You had two different crowds in there: in the day it was people who just wanted to place a quick bet and come back later if they won, and at night it was people who would hang out and watch a game together on TV.

That was where I got my first ever job. I was still just fifteen, but my dad had me working behind a counter, taking bets from the customers and handing out money to people who had won. I was also placing bets myself the whole time. I worked there for two years and never saw a single paycheck because the money always went straight to paying off bets I had made.

I really should have learned my lesson at that point because I saw people coming in every day and losing everything they had. But I didn't take that as a warning. I just found it unbelievably exciting, and every day there was a new opportunity for winning some big money. No two days were the same; there was always a new horse race or soccer game.

My dad didn't mind that I was betting. It was a thing we had together, and we would talk about the bets we made and the research we had done. That was a very interesting part of it for me, all the studying you did before placing a bet. It was like practice before playing in a game – you had to prepare yourself. Before betting on a soccer game, you would look to see which players were missing, who was injured, who was playing well. I spent a lot of time reading all the newspapers and soccer magazines. We didn't have the internet yet, so that information wasn't as easy to find as it is now – you had to put the time in.

The bookie wasn't the only place you could make a bet, though. Not long after I turned sixteen, I made my first trip to the local casino. It was small – nothing like the big ones you get in the United States – and it had not been there very long; the whole concept of casinos was still relatively new in Denmark. But *Oh my God,* it was exciting to see all that fast money in a place where you could win or lose a fortune in just a few seconds.

You weren't supposed to be allowed into the casino before the age of eighteen, but I managed to get a fake ID through an older friend. I went with him the first time, but later on I went with different friends and even my father. Dad had been going for a little while and it was because of him telling me about it that I got interested in the first place. I always found myself at the roulette table, because it was so fast; you found out almost immediately if you had won or lost.

I was also still playing soccer, of course. Soon after finishing with Norwich, I rejoined Aalborg, the club I had not played for since I was four years old and got hit in the face by that ball. I didn't get a contract there – even their senior players only got part-time salaries at that stage, as soccer in Denmark had always been semi-professional – but I would go there every evening to train with the academy.

Like I said, they were by far the biggest team in our area, with their senior team playing in Denmark's top division, the SuperLiga. It was nothing like the intensity and the competitiveness of Norwich, but it was more serious than B52, the club I had previously played for in Denmark.

It was fun to be involved with the team I had supported growing up. My father used to have season tickets to Aalborg when I was a little boy, and I would go with him to stand right behind the goal – like where the Cauldron is now at Sporting Park. My favorite part was always the warm-ups, and I would run down to the front and copy all the moves the Aalborg goalkeeper was doing. That was even more of a big deal for me than the game itself.

My return to playing for Aalborg did not go smoothly, though. Just a few weeks into my first preseason there, the academy coach, Poul Erik Kristensen, pulled me to one side and said, "Listen, you don't have the talent required to make it here. I think you should move back to B52 and have some fun, because this is a level too high for you. Maybe even three or four levels."

It was a horrible moment, a huge comedown after being offered a contract by Norwich. I don't know what made him think I wasn't good enough. Kit Carson was a great coach, and he clearly thought I had some talent. But everybody has their different opinions, and Aalborg already had a goalkeeper there at the time, Rune Carlsen, who Coach Kristensen obviously thought was better than me. I knew I couldn't go back to B52 after competing at such a high level with Norwich, so I persuaded him to let me stay around and play for the reserve team at my age category. It was after a practice session with them that my luck turned.

Aalborg's practice facility was a long way from where we lived, a good hour's drive, so my mom would usually come pick me up. One day she was running late, and I was sitting in the cafeteria waiting for her. I guess I must have been looking pretty down because the groundskeeper saw me and told me to come over and have a chat.

His name was Kaj Paulsen, and he was a former Aalborg goalkeeper who had even played a few games for the Danish national team. We sat down and he asked me what I was sad about. I told him about what Coach Kristensen had said and he simply replied, "Any time you want some coaching, you come to me. You don't have to pay anything, I will do this for free. I can see huge potential in you."

I was surprised to hear him say that since he didn't coach the team at all back then – he was just the groundskeeper – but I guess he must have been watching me while he was doing his work at the facility. He was certainly there a lot, coming in at 7:00 a.m. and not leaving till midnight some days. He was a ridiculously hard working guy.

From then on he became Coach Paulsen to me, and I would go train with him three, four, or even five times a week if I could. He was one of those guys who looked much older than he was, probably only in his late fifties but always walking around with hunched shoulders and his back bent over from working so hard all those years. But for those ninety minutes we were out practicing together, I swear to God he towered over the field and strode around like the strongest man who ever lived. His whole appearance seemed to change when we were out there with a soccer ball. It made him come alive.

He was very old-school in his methods, and when I look back now at some of what we did, it seems crazy. He would make me run up and down the hills near the training ground, carrying him on my back, or do another drill where he stood about a foot away from me and launched this enormous medicine ball into my stomach to make me stronger. But it worked. He made me grow up from a little boy into a young man.

After one season with the reserve team, I got promoted to play with the first-team again. I was playing well and Coach Kristensen had obviously changed his opinion of me. We actually got along very well by the end. When I became the starting goalkeeper for the senior Aalborg team a few years later, he was still working there, and I always reminded him about that day when he told me I wouldn't make it. Sadly, Coach Paulsen got sick and only saw me play a couple of games as a professional before he passed away. I was crushed when that happened; he meant so much to me. He was the one who showed faith in me when I needed it most.

You're probably wondering at this point how I managed to play all this soccer and work at the bookie while I was still in high school. The truth is that I dropped out at the end of seventh grade, which is the earliest point at which you are allowed to leave the education system in Denmark. I was still just fifteen, and my mom was so sad. She begged me to keep on going for another couple of years, but I just wasn't interested.

In reality, I had given up on school long before that point. It was ridiculous really. My mom stopped me from joining Norwich because she wanted me to focus on my studies, but that whole last year I was skipping more classes than I attended. I would play hooky when I wanted to go train with Coach Paulsen, but I also did it at times when I didn't have anybody to play with.

Some days I would just go find somewhere to kick a ball up against a wall on my own. I used to drive our neighbors crazy doing that. I could happily stay in one place for thirty minutes, knocking the ball up against the wall of the house until the lady who lived there would come out and say, "Jimmy! You've got to stop now. All my pictures are falling off their hooks." Then I would go around the corner, find another wall and stay there until whoever lived in that house came out and told me to stop. I could keep moving on like that all morning. There was always a place where I could do something with a soccer ball. It was the same in the evening: if for whatever reason there was no soccer going on in that big park by my home, there were a few other smaller places I knew where I could try to find a game. That was my life, chasing soccer.

When I was 15 years old, my coach at Aalborg, Poul Erik Kristensen, told me I wasn't going to make it as a soccer player and that I would be better off finding a less competitive team to play for. Two years later, here he is giving me the team's Player of the Season award.

At first, the teachers called home to tell my parents that I was skipping school. My mom would always get upset – not angry, just really disappointed – and I would promise her that it wasn't going to happen again, but then a few days later it always did. After a while, the school just stopped calling.

The way I behaved is not something to be proud of, and I know I would be disappointed if my kids did the same thing. But I also cannot say I have any regrets about it because everything I did back then is part of who I am today. Playing soccer was fun, and it kept me out of trouble. I still say I was a pretty good kid. I didn't drink or do drugs or get into fights. The only thing I really got in trouble for was skipping classes to play soccer. I think there are worse things that a teenager can get involved in.

Like gambling, I suppose.

6
GOING PRO

Sometimes it's the tiny decisions that change your life. That was certainly the case for me in the summer of 1994. I was leaving my parents' apartment one afternoon and had just finished locking the door when I heard the phone inside start to ring. I stood there for a moment, listening and wondering if I could really be bothered to undo those locks again just to run in and probably miss the call anyway. It was one of those situations where 50% of the time I'm going to ignore it and walk away, but that day, for whatever reason, I went back in to find the phone.

"Hey, is that Jimmy?" said the voice on the other end of the line. "This is Peter Andersen, the Danish Under-17 national team coach. We're playing a tournament in Belgium and we need another goalkeeper. Can you be on a plane in a few hours' time?"

I was thinking, *Oh, come on.* I didn't know where all of my things were. I wasn't ready, and I was supposed to be meeting some people in town a few minutes later. But this was the first time I had ever been called up by the national team, and I wasn't about to turn that down. I told him, "Yes. I will be there." Five hours later, I was in Belgium.

Just like with Norwich a few years earlier, the starting goalkeeper was sick, so they needed me to play straight away in the opening game of the tournament. It was against Wales. I know I had a good game, but I couldn't tell you the exact score. The coach told me afterwards that he was really impressed, so I got to stay on the team for the second game and then the third one, too. The last game was against Holland, which is traditionally much better at soccer than Denmark. We won 4-0.

That was a huge result for us, and from then on I was the starting goalkeeper, at first for the Under-17 team, and later, the U-18, U-19 and U-21 teams. It wasn't just the national team coaches who were impressed. A few European soccer teams were scouting that tournament, and immediately afterward, Millwall, an English club, got in touch. They invited me over to take part in a two-week trial.

Millwall, based in south London, was playing in the second-highest division at that time, but it had just built a new 20,000-seat stadium, so it was a similar-sized club to Norwich. The scout told me they needed a reserve goalkeeper for their senior team, which sounded like a pretty big deal to a kid who was still a few weeks away from turning seventeen.

I hated that trial, though. Millwall put me up in a bed & breakfast just like the one I had stayed in when Norwich forgot to pick me up at the airport, bringing back all of the bad memories from that trip. South London had some tough neighborhoods then, too, so it was not a place where you felt completely safe if you didn't know your way around.

The soccer itself was fine, but I was the youngest player there by a very long way – maybe as much as eight or nine years – and the

My first call-up to the Danish Under-17 national team couldn't have gone much better. It was for a small tournament in Belgium, and I got named as the best goalkeeper in the whole competition. My prize was a Camel watch, which I'm holding in this picture. I wore it for years, but I have no idea where it is now.

atmosphere was very different from Norwich. These guys were veterans who had played through tough careers, and they were hard and cynical. They weren't mean to me, but they didn't go out of their way to make me feel welcome, either, and it was hard for me as a sixteen-year-old kid with bad English to start up a conversation.

Millwall didn't have a goalkeeping coach at that time, so the only thing we did for those two weeks was shooting practice. The team's forwards would take turns to have shots, and I just had to try to save them. I wasn't enjoying myself, but it clearly didn't affect my performance, because right when I was about to return to Aalborg, they decided to offer me a contract.

It was pretty generous offer for a sixteen-year-old kid – £1,500 (about $2,250) per week salary plus a signing bonus of £200,000 ($300,000). Even so, I wasn't sure I wanted to accept it. Those two weeks had been pretty miserable, so I told them I would have to go away and think about it.

On the day I was due to leave, the team's manager, Mick McCarthy, drove me to the airport, along with the scout who first spotted me playing for the Denmark U-17 team. After I checked in for my flight, we all went and sat down in a bar before I went through to departures. They were talking to me a little more about why they thought Millwall would be a good fit, telling me I could have a great future there, and out of nowhere, the team's chairman showed up.

He was this really old guy in a big jacket, and he came into the bar about ten minutes before they were set to start boarding my plane. He walked straight over and said he had heard great things about me from McCarthy and that he was surprised I hadn't signed the contract yet, adding that if it was about money, he would raise his offer right there and then. I said "no, no, no" – because it really wasn't about that for me. I couldn't bring myself to tell them that I just didn't like it there.

So for the next few minutes, he was telling me all about the club, its history, and its ambitions to get up to the top division – a lot of the same stuff that I had already talked about with McCarthy. After that, it was finally time for me to leave, but as I got up to go, the chairman stopped me.

"Do you have any money on you?" he asked.

"Yeah, I have a few pounds."

"Here, take this..."

He stuck his hand in his pocket and pulled out a huge wad of bills. I don't know how much it was exactly, but if I had to guess, I'd say at least four or five hundred pounds. It was all in twenties, so it looked like even more than it was. My eyes must have popped out of my head as I stared at all that money. It was ridiculous; I had to be on a plane a few minutes later and there was no way I could spend that amount in the airport before I left. But now I truly understood how much they wanted me.

I had another trial lined up with Borussia Monchengladbach, a top-division team from Germany, which had also seen me during that tournament for the U-17s. Pretty much as soon as I got back to Denmark, I had to fly out there. That was only for a few days, but I enjoyed the trial went even less than the one at Millwall. If my English was poor, my German was a whole lot worse, so there was no way for me to communicate with people. Borussia Monchengladbach never tried to sign me afterward, so I guess they didn't think much of me.

Aalborg must have caught wind of the situation. They tried to offer me a contract at that point, sending me a proposal on the very day I got back from Germany. But by that point I'd decided that I should go to Millwall, partly because my dad kept telling me it might be the only opportunity I had to sign for an important club in Britain and that there was no guarantee I would have the chance to be a pro later down the line. But it was also because I could see how badly Millwall wanted me. They just kept calling and calling. Although we never asked for more money, they said yes to anything else we asked for, whether it was arranging an apartment for me or hiring someone to come round a few times per week to cook and clean.

So at seventeen, I moved out of my parents' house and into an apartment in south London. Just like I had told Ms. Else in her little classroom all those years before, I was going to live my dream of being a professional soccer player.

7
AN ENGLISH ADVENTURE

The thing nobody tells you about being a professional soccer player is how much free time you're going to have. You wake up in the morning, you go to practice, you have lunch, maybe you attend a few team meetings after that, but otherwise, unless the coach has ordered double sessions or you have a game in the evening, the rest of the day is yours.

That time is a dangerous thing to have when you are a seventeen-year-old living far away from your friends and family. My parents still had their jobs, so it wasn't like either of them could come over for any extended period, and my dad won't fly, so it was difficult for him to visit at the best of times. It was also hard for me to make new friends since there was nobody on the team my age.

Inevitably, I found myself filling up that spare time at the place where I felt most comfortable: the betting shop. There was one very near my house, a branch of the big British bookie William Hill, a national chain with shops all over the country. It was a small store with a big blue sign over the door and lots of TVs inside where you could watch all the different sports you might want to bet on.

I became a regular visitor there shortly after I arrived. I had betting in my blood from all those horse races in Denmark and from working in my dad's bookie, so it was nothing new to me. Now, though, I could go whenever I wanted, without anybody controlling me or looking over my shoulder. It was so comfortable. Every day that I walked in there I just felt like *ahhhhhhh, I'm home.*

After a while, I started to make friends there. Well, maybe you wouldn't call them friends, but certainly I had my gambling buddies.

55

Every day it would be the same people, and we could sit and talk for hours about a single soccer game that was coming up that evening. I've told you how I liked to do my research before placing a bet, and this was like an extension of that, hearing different opinions and things that each person had read.

I could change my mind about what bet I was going to place five times in the last ten minutes before a game kicked off, but eventually I would put my money on, and then we would sit and watch it together. Just like the kids I played soccer with at Norwich, these people reminded me of myself. Perhaps it was in a different way, but they were all extremely competitive. They all wanted to win.

Maybe I needed that outlet a little bit more than before, too, because I was not getting to play any games for Millwall. I did very well in practice to begin with, but it wasn't a satisfying experience. As I already knew from my trial, there was no goalkeeping coach, so every day was just the same thing over and over, facing shots from the forwards.

Practice at Millwall got pretty repetitive because we didn't have a goalkeeping coach. All we ever did was go up against the forwards in shooting practice. Fans of English soccer might recognize the guy in the middle of this photo – it's Ben Thatcher, who went on to play for Wimbledon, Tottenham Hotspur and a few other clubs.

Millwall's starting goalie at that time was Kasey Keller, a player most readers will know well and who went on to play more than 100 games for the United States national team. He was a fantastic goalkeeper and an extremely nice guy. He gave me pointers about my technique, but I know he was just as annoyed as I was about the lack of a coach, and he was always asking management to do something about it.

There was one time when Kasey really helped me out off of the pitch. Not long after I moved to England, I was out one afternoon when my bank card got swallowed by the ATM. Your paycheck didn't go straight into your account there – it was a physical check you had to take to the bank and wait a few days for the money to appear. I had paid mine in but it was still not showing up. I had no money, and now this machine had taken my card as well.

I'd just received my first cell phone – they were still brand new back then – and Kasey's was the only English number I had stored on it. I called him up and said, "I'm so sorry to bother you, Kasey, but this happened and I don't know what to do." He just asked where I lived and said, "OK, I'll be there in an hour." And he was, just as he promised.

He lent me £500 ($750), and told me just to pay him back when I could. A few days later, I finally managed to get some money out of the bank and went straight to the training ground to give it to him. He said, "Don't worry about it, you keep it. But in the future, be careful with your money." That was some advice I probably should have taken.

Unfortunately, Kasey being at Millwall also meant I had no chance of getting a game for the senior team. He was playing really well, and I was not even certain of getting a place on the bench – the rules at that time only allowed teams to have three substitutes each. Because it's so rare that you lose your goalie during a game, sometimes Mick McCarthy would choose outfield players for all three.

It's not an original thought, but goalkeeper really is the worst position on the team to be a back-up. Nobody changes their goalie after 60 minutes, so even if you are on the bench, the only way you're going to play is if the guy ahead of you gets hurt or gets a red card. And if it's a guy you train with every day, someone you get on with, you don't exactly sit on the bench wishing misfortune on him.

I was there at the wrong time. I'm very impatient and I don't like sitting around wasting my time. Millwall knew that sooner or later they were going to sell Kasey, so the idea was for me to become his eventual replacement. But it was hard to sit there and be the reserve, never playing games and not even getting good coaching.

I was really unhappy after a few months, so I asked the academy coach, Tom Walley, if I could start playing with the youth team. He spoke to Mick McCarthy who said it was okay. I had a much better time there, and I started to have fun again with kids who were the same age as me.

On one occasion, I was traveling to an away game with the youth team. We started making little paper balls to throw at the equipment manager whose name I can no longer remember. Coach Walley always used to travel separately, so this equipment manager was the only adult on the bus besides the driver. After a few seconds of having these paper balls thrown at him, he jumped up, turned around and said, "Jimmy, stop doing that!" He used a few other words, too, which I won't repeat here.

I said, "It's not me, I didn't do anything." It was a lie, but I certainly wasn't the only one. A few minutes later I started getting ready to do it again, but just as I was about to throw that ball, I made eye contact with him in the rear view mirror. He didn't say a word, so I just sat back down and forgot about it.

The following Monday, one of the assistants at training grabbed me and said, "Jimmy, the gaffer wants a word." So I walked into Mick McCarthy's office feeling very happy – we'd had a good game that weekend – and said hi, but he just said, "Sit down." Then he absolutely lost it on me – he went crazy. He was swearing and shouting at me, using words I didn't even know. I got fined a week's wages for the paper ball episode, which, as I've explained, was not a small amount of money. They were very big on discipline with the young players at Millwall, which I actually quite approve of. Kids need a hard line sometimes.

That was not the only time I got fined at Millwall. On another occasion, our reserve team had a game against Tottenham and I was on the bench. By halftime we were losing 5-0, and we came into the locker room totally silent because we were getting absolutely destroyed. Mick McCarthy didn't always watch the reserve games, but he was there that day, suddenly showing up at the door of the locker room with a face like thunder.

He started screaming, tearing into us. I hadn't been on the pitch, so it wasn't really aimed at me, but it was still pretty scary. All of a sudden, my phone started ringing. I had my pants hanging up on the peg next to where I was sitting and I could hear it going *brrring-brrring-brrrring*. For some stupid reason, I went to answer it. I could see on the display that it was my mom calling, so I picked it up and I just tried to whisper, "I'm going to have to call back later."

Even as I was saying that, I could hear that the room had gone quiet. Mick McCarthy was standing there, staring at me in silence. Finally, he spoke.

"Let me have a look at that phone."

I handed it straight to him without even hanging up the call. He took it from me, looked at it for a second, and then *Boom!* – he threw it as hard as he could onto the floor. He absolutely killed it, smashed it into 1,000 pieces. I got fined another £500 for that, although my mom felt so guilty about it she wound up paying it for me.

But I don't want to give the impression that I had a bad relationship with Mick McCarthy. Many years later when I was back in England with Leicester City, he tried to get me to come and play for him at Wolves. It didn't work out because we were already too close to the end to the transfer window, but he obviously didn't mind having me around.

And Tom Walley certainly liked having me in the academy. He had been in rehab for gambling addiction and was supposed to have stopped, but nobody told me about that when I first arrived. So when he figured out that I was going down to the bookie regularly, he started asking me to place bets for him. He would come over to me shouting, "Hey, Jimmy. This horse, in this race, is a sure-fire winner. Put your money on, put this much money on for me as well, and I'll bring you the money tomorrow at training."

The horse would lose, of course, but I was never brave enough to go to him and ask for the money he owed me. After a little while, one of the parents of the kids in the academy must have seen what was going on because they came and told me about his background.

I was beginning to have my own problems, too. Even before I arrived in England, I had begun lying to cover up how much I was gambling. Back in Denmark, I kept my fake ID and my trips to the casino a secret not only from my mom, but from some of the friends who might accidentally let it slip to her if I told them.

But now that I was in London on my own, it was so much easier to hide things from the people who might have worried about me. After I had dropped down to play with the academy, I was training with kids my age again, and sometimes they would invite me out for dinner or to catch a movie or something. But I would make up excuses to get out of it so that I could go to the bookie instead, saying I had plans or that someone was coming to visit me from Denmark.

Even if I did tell people that I was gambling on a certain game or a particular race, I wouldn't tell them how much the bet was for. If I put £500 on a game, I would also place a separate £10 bet on the same thing. That way, I could tell people why I was excited about a particular horse or team and could celebrate if I won, without having to tell them how much I was risking.

It was definitely getting out of hand. There was one time when I was supposed to be flying back to Denmark very early in the morning, but, as per usual, I had been at the bookie the night before. I had gone to the ATM on my way there and had taken out the maximum I was allowed – a few hundred pounds – but I purposely set aside £60 to pay for my cab to the airport.

So I went to the bookie, and it was one of those nights where I just kept on losing, couldn't seem to hit a winner. Eventually, the only thing I had left was that £60 to get me to the airport. I stood there looking at that money and thought: *This is for the cab.* But I just couldn't stop myself making another bet. And it lost.

The next morning, I was trying to figure out a story to tell the cab driver, and I didn't say anything until we had almost got to the airport. Just when it was coming into view, I started patting all my pockets and acting very anxious, and then I told him, "Oh my God, I haven't got any money on me." He immediately slammed on the brakes.

"*WHAT?*"

I was pretty lucky that the guy who had come to pick me up that day was someone who drove me a lot, but he was still furious. I told him that if he came to get me when I returned, I could pay him then, but he said that wasn't good enough. I eventually managed to convince him that I would have the money transferred as soon as I got to Denmark. Thankfully, my mom was able to do that for me.

I should have heard the alarm bells ringing by that stage, but instead I allowed things to get more and more serious. What started out as £10 bets became £15, then £20, then more and more until it was up in the hundreds every day.

It wasn't like I was losing all the time; there were big wins, too. One night at Millwall, I went to the casino on my own and won £25,000 ($37,500) playing roulette. But because I was keeping everything a secret, I had nobody to celebrate it with. I just went home that night and stuck the money in my closet. The problem with winning that amount of money is that the next time you go to the casino you have to bet even more because it's not fun anymore to go there and win £500. You always have to go bigger.

But, you know, everybody had their own problems. I was very surprised when I got to England and found out how many of the players – and I mean the academy players as well – would go out drinking after practice. Some of them would sit in the pub drinking beer all afternoon, and that was just normal, everybody did it.

I didn't drink – gambling was what gave me my boost. But I have always said that if an alcoholic (and I don't mean to suggest my teammates were all alcoholics, but just to make the general point) felt the same way about having a beer as I did about having a bet, then I completely understand. I would sit there and panic, thinking, *I'm not going to make that bet, I'm not going to make that bet,* but the second I gave in and did it, my whole body would relax. It was just like, *ahhhhhh…*

Not that I thought I was addicted back then. Gambling was just my release, my hobby, something to do during all those long hours when I wasn't playing soccer. And it has to be said that the longer I stayed at Millwall, the more it felt like the soccer itself was not going very well.

I had signed for Millwall in the summer of 1994, but by the end of my first season it was already clear things were not working out. I had a training camp with the Denmark U-17 team sometime in February, and I was playing really badly. The coach pulled me to one side when we were getting ready to go home and told me that he wouldn't be able to keep calling me up unless something changed. I was going backward at Millwall because we didn't have a goalkeeping coach and I wasn't getting any help with my technique.

The one chance I did get with the Millwall senior team was a total disaster. We were playing in a tournament. I can't remember what it was called, but it was something really minor. The teams from the top division weren't involved, and I don't think they even included appearances from that tournament in the club's official statistics at the end of the season, so it was almost more like an exhibition.

But this particular game was against Crystal Palace, one of Millwall's biggest rivals. So even though the tournament didn't matter, the game itself was still a big deal to the fans. We were playing at Crystal Palace's stadium, Selhurst Park, but there were several hundred of our supporters who had gone down to see the game.

Up until the 85th minute, I had no doubt I would be the game's MVP. I was playing really well, I had made some important saves and we were winning 1-0. Then with five minutes left, I gave away a stupid penalty. The forward had come running in toward me, but his touch was so bad that he had to turn away just to get control of the ball. Instead of moving toward the goal, he was now running away from it, but for some crazy reason, I decided to slide tackle him from behind. He went down, and the referee pointed to the spot.

Of course they scored the PK, and in overtime I made another mistake. We lost the game 2-1, and I had the Millwall fans right behind my goal. They had a reputation as some of the roughest fans in England, and they were not about to forgive me for that mistake. They started singing: "The goalie is a wanker! The goalie is a wanker!"

By the time I got down to the locker room afterwards, I felt horrible. I was hoping my teammates might feel a little sorry for me – you know, I was a kid, and this was my first game with the senior team – but instead they were all cursing at me, saying, "You are useless" and much worse than that.

Locker rooms at soccer grounds all had big baths in them back then – a lot of them still do – so I went down there to soak and get away a little bit. I sat in there for a little while just thinking, *Oh my God, I feel awful.* Finally I climbed out and went to get dressed, but I quickly realized there was nobody else in the locker room. I was thinking, *OK, I better hurry up or they're going to be mad at me for making them wait on the bus.* But when I came out, I couldn't find the bus at all. I asked the security guy, "Where is the Millwall bus?" and he said, "They left ten minutes ago."

I couldn't believe it. Nobody had come into the locker room to tell me to hurry up or to warn me that the bus was about to leave. Instead, they had clearly just said, "Screw him. He can get back on his own."

It was a local derby, so at least I could get home. I caught a cab and then took a day off like we always had after games. The next Monday, I came back in to the team facility. Almost as soon as I got there I ran into Mick McCarthy. "What the hell are you doing here?" he said.

"I'm here for practice."

"I don't want to look at you. I don't want to see your face here. You're going home."

He was yelling by this point, so loudly that everybody stopped what they were doing to watch.

"What do you mean I'm going home?"

"I don't want to see your face here. Get a ticket back to Denmark."

I wanted to defend myself. Beyond having played a bad game, I didn't really see what I had done wrong. But it was pretty clear that he wasn't going to listen. I had a lot of respect for Mick McCarthy – he was a good coach and he'd had a great playing career – but he was also a pretty scary guy. I had seen him screaming right in the faces of the toughest players on that Millwall team, making them run until they were physically sick in practice and then ordering them to get up and keep going, with the vomit still fresh on their shirts.

So there was not a lot of point in arguing. I asked him when I was supposed to come back to practice, and he just said, "When you get a phone call." So I went home, packed a bag, and got on a plane to Denmark the same night.

Two days later, on Wednesday afternoon, I got a call from one of the team assistants. He told me the manager wanted me back the next morning, but by that point it was already too late to catch a flight. I tried calling the travel agent and the airport, but nothing could be done. I called the assistant back to tell him, but he just said, "You better be here tomorrow morning for practice."

Of course I didn't make it, and so, after getting shouted at again, I was handed another fine. A few days later, I was on the bench for another senior team game, this time at home, and as soon as I walked out onto the field, the fans started booing and shouting abuse. At that point I knew I was done. I think everyone else at the club did, too.

Things moved pretty quickly after that. I called my dad and told him how unhappy I was, and he just said, "Go and tell the manager everything you told me." So I went to Mick McCarthy the next day. We had a really calm conversation about it all, and he said, "That's fine, you can go. But we want back the money we paid for you." He was referring to the signing bonus, which as I mentioned, was a good $300,000. The problem was that I didn't have it all. I had already gambled away more than $60,000.

That was a doubly difficult position because my parents didn't know how much I had been betting, and now I found myself lying to them about what had happened to that money, saying I had spent it on nice meals or whatever. I told them I gambled some of it, but I didn't want them to know how much. It would have been easier if I had at least bought something big like a car or a house, but I hadn't done anything like that.

Still, I must have gotten away with it because I don't remember them getting angry with me. Instead, a few days later, my dad and sister came over to England (He managed to find a way that didn't involve getting on a plane!) and went to speak to Mick McCarthy on my behalf. My sister's English was unbelievable, because unlike me, she actually paid attention in school. They went in there and had a long discussion with the manager, who eventually agreed to just take what was left of my signing bonus.

And so that was that, my English adventure was over as quickly as it had begun. By the time I flew back to Denmark in December 1995, we had already found a team over there, Viborg, who wanted me. But just as I was about to sign a deal with them, my old club, Aalborg, came in with an offer. Their starting goalkeeper had just left and they wanted me to come in and compete for the job.

The timing was perfect. After a year of feeling lost and homesick in a foreign country, what could be better than coming back home to play for the club I supported as a boy?

I never did like sitting on the bench, but I wound up doing quite a lot of that at Millwall. At least it wasn't as cold in England as it was back in Denmark.

8
'THE NEXT PETER SCHMEICHEL'

$O\mathcal{N}$ my first day with Aalborg, I stood beside manager Sepp Piontek as he introduced me to the local press. I was one of the first players the club had ever signed to a full-time contract, since soccer in Denmark had previously always been a semi-professional sport. The money, about 12,000 Danish Krone ($2,100) per month, was nothing compared to what I had been making at Millwall, but I was still feeling pretty good about myself as he began to sing my praises.

"Now I must show you our newest arrival," Piontek said. "He is a fantastic, talented young goalkeeper who comes to us from... erm... his name is... umm..."

He paused for a few seconds. Slowly, it began to dawn on me: my new manager had absolutely no idea who I was. Finally, he turned back and started whispering.

"Hey, what is your name?"

I was thinking, *Is this a test? Surely this can't be real*, but he was right there, staring at me from just a few inches away, so I had to say something.

"It's Jimmy Nielsen," I whispered back.

Obviously he didn't hear me well, because instead of telling the reporters my name, he just turned back and started comparing me to the greatest Danish goalkeeper of all time.

"Yes, this is the next Peter Schmeichel – like I said, a very talented young man. I'm sure you will be seeing a lot of him very soon."

Schmeichel was a legend in Denmark, the starting goalkeeper for Manchester United and arguably the best in the world at that time. Three years before my arrival in Aalborg, he helped the Danish national team to win its first-ever major international tournament, the

1992 European Championships in Sweden. Even people who didn't care about soccer knew who Peter Schmeichel was. My own teammates had no idea who I might be.

The comparison with Schmeichel was one I would hear plenty more times over the next few years. We're both tall, we're both Danish, and we both have blonde hair, which was enough for most people. Unfortunately, I'm not on the same planet as him when it comes to playing soccer. The good news is that I am a little more handsome!

As for Sepp Piontek, that turned out to be how he was all of the time. He was an incredibly confusing man, always changing subject mid-sentence and interrupting training sessions so that he could tell stories or make jokes. He was very funny and motivating. The players all loved him, and you woke up excited to go to practice every morning because you didn't know what was going to happen next.

He got fired about six months after I arrived, though, because the team was not living up to expectations in the league. He was replaced by Per Westergaard at first, but Aalborg went through a lot of different

This is the day I got introduced to the media after signing for Aalborg, my hometown club. The guy standing with me is my new manager, Sepp Piontek, and if he looks a bit confused, it's probably because he has no idea who I am! Moments before this shot was taken, he had introduced me to reporters as "the next Peter Schmeichel" because he couldn't remember my real name.

managers over the next few years. To be honest, none of that was as important to me as having a good goalkeeping coach. As I mentioned, the Danish U-17 coach had warned me that I was going backward at Millwall, so I needed somebody who would get back to basics with me and give me some practice drills that went beyond just stopping shots.

I found what I was looking for in Aalborg. They had just appointed Harbo Larsen, who was the team's starting goalkeeper through much of my childhood. It was fun getting coached by the guy whose warm-ups I used to copy from behind the goal. I remembered all his biggest games, and I always used to tease him about a penalty he gave away in the 1987 Danish Cup final. I probably shouldn't have, because we went on to have some pretty bad luck in that competition ourselves.

Harbo was a very good coach. He was very serious, never sloppy and always well-prepared. We worked hard when we were out on the field, and there was no time for joking around, which made for a sharp contrast with Piontek. Most importantly, he understood the techniques and skills that were required to be a great goalkeeper, and he was very good at communicating those things to us.

He was also a good man off the field, always talking to me about how to live right and look after my body. Unfortunately, we never spoke about gambling (I was good at hiding that from people), but he did teach me a lot about how to carry myself and behave in front of Aalborg's media spotlight. Whenever I did or said something he wasn't happy about, he would let me know straight away, and I always listened.

For the first year I was at Aalborg, I served as the backup for the senior team. As I mentioned in the last chapter, the starting goalkeeper, a Norwegian international named Thomas Gill, had just left, but his backup, Lars Winde, replaced him in the lineup. He was another young Danish guy, just a couple of years older than me. He was playing well, but I still felt like I had a chance to win that job from him.

My first chance came early in that first season, after Lars suffered an ankle injury. We were on the road against Ikast. I went out onto the field, did my warm-ups, mixed in a few of those moves I learned watching Harbo, and went back down into the locker room to get ready and have the team talk. I was not at all nervous, just really excited to play. But my biggest memory of the day is when we came back out of the tunnel to start the match, the whole pitch was covered in snow. That had not been the case when we went inside five minutes earlier. Apparently, a crazy blizzard had set in the second we stepped inside.

Playing in the snow is the most difficult thing for a goalkeeper. Not only is the ball impossible to hold, but you never know how it's going to bounce. Sometimes it will skid and travel at 100mph, other times it hits a pile of snow and just dies. We had to play with a bright orange ball so that the players would be able to see it against all that white. The first time I held it in my hands it felt like a piece of wet soap.

I stood there thinking, *This is going to be crazy*, but in the end it worked out okay. We tied 1-1, and I didn't really have a lot to do because my team was playing well. I made a couple of saves, and there wasn't a lot I could have done about Ikast's goal – it was a smart finish right into the top corner.

Lars came back into the team after that and played the rest of the season, so it wasn't until the next year that I replaced him. I got my chance after he suffered another injury, this time to his shoulder. He was out for a few weeks, and I played so well that they let me keep the job once he had recovered. I never looked back, and I went on to start a club record 398 consecutive games over the next eleven years.

I am incredibly proud of what I achieved with the team I had supported growing up. I had some great times at Aalborg, twice getting the team MVP and twice getting Danish Goalkeeper of the Year award. But I have to admit that, for the first few years, I was not always very focused on my career there. I was working hard in practice, but because I was playing well and getting compared to Peter Schmeichel, there were constant reports in the papers linking me with a transfer away to some big club in England, Italy or Spain.

In the buildup to every game we played there would always be a headline like: "Today Southampton is here to watch Nielsen" or, "Everton is here to watch Nielsen today." I caught myself during the games thinking about it. If I had a good save, I'd wonder if the scout had seen it. If I made a mistake, I'd spend the next five minutes thinking: *Oh man, I hope he was in the restroom*. I was still enjoying my soccer, but

I was spending too much time worrying about who was watching me that day, where I was going to live or which team I might be playing for in the next transfer window.

It all came to a head a few years later, in 1999. I was playing for the Denmark Under-21 team against England, in Bradford. Before that game, it was all over the newspapers that Alex Ferguson, the Manchester United manager, was coming down to watch me. Peter Schmeichel had just left United a few months earlier, so this idea that the 'next Schmeichel' was coming to play a game in front of Ferguson made for a great story.

Of course, I had read all of those reports. I went out onto the pitch thinking that this was my big chance because Ferguson was not the only one watching. There were a lot of other scouts from different English teams, and I was 'in the shop window,' as they like to say over there. But instead of being the day my dreams came true, it turned out to be an absolute nightmare. We lost 4-1, and I was awful, really awful. It was not like I had one really obvious, gigantic mistake, but on any other afternoon, I would have saved at least two of those goals.

After the game, I went straight in for a shower before going directly onto the bus. The team's administrator boarded and said, "There are a few journalists here who want to talk to you." So I got off the bus and was surrounded by reporters from all the big English newspapers, asking, "Do you think Fergie was pleased with what he saw today?" I don't remember exactly what I said, but it was something along the lines of: "If Fergie saw me today, he's probably never going to sign me." And guess what? I was right!

I remember reading all the reports about how bad I had been in that game. These days when I make a mistake, I will go and watch it on TV over and over again to see what I could have done better, but I really don't care what the newspapers say. Back then I was different, much more sensitive, so I always wanted to read what rating they gave me. I'm sure I was something like a 4 out of 10 in that game.

Looking back, I don't even know why I thought it would be a good idea to leave – given how badly things had gone for me at Millwall – but I guess I got caught up a little bit in the numbers as well. Every time the newspapers were talking about one of these transfers, they would report that Aalborg was going to demand $3m for me, or $5m, or $7m. I would read that and think: *Wow, I'm going to make a lot of money here!*

I don't know if that was an excuse for me, but it definitely didn't help with my gambling. I was always thinking that I'd make some big money in the next few months or few years. And even though that transfer never materialized, Aalborg kept tearing up my contract every season and giving me a better one as a reward for playing well.

I have to thank the team's general manager, Lynge Jakobsen, for that. He arrived at the club just after me, in early 1996, but right away we had a fantastic relationship. Lynge was an incredibly charismatic guy, the sort who could talk to anybody. It wouldn't have mattered if he was in a room with President Obama or a group of homeless people, by the time he left, everybody would be raving about what an amazing guy he was.

I realize that sounds a bit like my dad, and it's probably a fair comparison. At Aalborg, a lot of my teammates started referring to Lynge and me as father-and-son. We had that sort of relationship where I felt like I could go to him with my problems, and I knew he was always going to stick up for me in public whilst being completely honest behind closed doors. He was not afraid of giving out advice on or off the field, and he was an unbelievable listener. You got his 100% attention, and he didn't rush to judgments. If you came to him with a problem, you knew he would go away and keep thinking about what could be done after that conversation finished, rather than just trying to come up with the quickest solution that might not be the best. When life got tough for me a little later on, he was an incredible help.

For now, though, I was gambling all the time, even if I had to reduce the size of the bets a little bit to start with. My salary was lower, so I had to adjust, but I kept on pushing the limits of what I could afford. At first I went back to my dad's bookie, but he closed that down not long after I got back. It was a great place to spend time, but it was not a good business for a guy like my dad, who was gambling regularly himself. Right away, I found a new bookie with a similar atmosphere that worked better for me because now my dad wouldn't know how much I was gambling.

After initially moving back in with my parents, I soon got my own apartment. Again, that made the gambling easier, as I didn't have to tell anyone what I was doing with my time. I started going back to the old casino, not every now and then, but four, five, six times a week. I had a few different friends I would go with so that I could switch up each night, to the point that even they didn't know how often I was going.

We had some long nights in there. My credit card had a limit which restricted how much I could withdraw each day, but if I held out until midnight, I could take out the same amount again. I cannot tell you how many times I sat in that casino at 11pm with no money in my pockets, waiting that next hour for the clock to hit midnight so I could start gambling again.

I built up debts straight away, but the banks were always happy to loan money to young soccer players with promising careers ahead of them. Of course I didn't tell them what the money was for. Let's just say I "changed my curtains" and "got a new bathroom" more often in those years at Aalborg than most people do in a whole lifetime. I was borrowing from different banks at different times. Even so, those guys must have thought I was crazy obsessed with home furnishings.

Gambling is like being on a rollercoaster – you always have ups and downs – and there were times when I was doing well enough for all those debts to be cleared. The bad spells never lasted long enough for me to worry that I might not find a way back. Life was good. I was living and playing soccer in my hometown, and I felt so much happier than I ever did at Millwall.

It was fun playing in front of the crowd that I used to be a part of, and when I came out on the field for our home games, I would see kids behind the goal copying my moves like I used to do with Harbo. I tried to get out there a little early sometimes so I could have a chat with them and give them some tips.

The rest of the crowd was not always so easy to please. Aalborg has some very passionate supporters, and when you're doing well, the atmosphere is unbelievable. The stadium can only hold a little less than 15,000, but it would be full every game. When you're winning, they make you feel incredible, but when you start losing, they turn against you like lightning. After a run of bad results, you would see images on TV of twenty guys getting together and setting fire to their replica jerseys, which was good news for the club shop because those same fans would always be back for the next game, wearing the new jerseys they had bought.

There was a story from the 2011-12 season – long after I had left – that says a lot about how much the soccer team means to that city. Aalborg was supposed to be playing one evening, but it had been snowing heavily. At 2:00 p.m. on the day of the game, the referee took one look at the pitch and said, "There is no way we are going to play." The club put out an announcement on its website saying that if 100 people didn't show up with shovels to clear the pitch, the game would be canceled. An hour later there were 200 people moving that snow, and there were more outside who got turned away because there wasn't any room for them on the field. The game was played.

It was a great place to work, too, with good, hardworking people throughout the organization. Plus in that first year, I got to play very briefly with my all-time favorite player, a midfielder named Søren

Our fans at Aalborg were certainly passionate. This guy got so worked up that he ran onto the field, and I had to help escort him back off. I remember this game well, because about a minute after the guy left, a naked woman ran onto the pitch and came sprinting down toward my goal. I decided I was better off letting the security guards look after her!

Thorst. He got injured in my first season and wound up retiring after that (though he later came back as an assistant coach), but it was amazing to be on the same team with him, even if it was only for a little while. When I was a kid, my Aalborg shirt always had his name on the back.

His nickname was "the Scissors" because he would come in and chop your legs off. I admired the hell out of him. He wasn't the greatest player on the pitch, but he was there 100% in every single game. He was a hard, tough but fair player. You could see his passion for the game every time he stepped out onto that field. That has always been the thing I want to see most in a soccer player: that love for the game, like I always had.

But the other nice thing about being back in Aalborg was getting to spend a little more time with my granny. She had been very sick over the previous five years and had been in and out of the hospital with cancer and a terrible gastric ulcer, which meant she wasn't really supposed to drink coffee, though she allowed herself one if she had visitors.

I used to call her every day back when I was at Millwall, but it was much better to see each other in person. Her apartment was on the third floor, and as you will remember, she was walking around on crutches even when I was a little boy. But now it was hard for her to get downstairs on her own, so whenever I came to visit, she would say, "Oh, I'm dying to get out for five or ten minutes." I would help her down the stairs and we would go for a walk in the old park. No soccer this time, though!

Granny was an unbelievable lady, so strong. She raised my dad and three other kids on her own, working as a sewing machinist in a big factory. And she did well. She was not rich by the end, but she certainly wasn't poor. When my dad wanted $10,000 to start his first bar, she was the one who lent it to him.

But she didn't need those last five years of her life. Granny was in a lot of pain, and when she finally passed away in February, I was sad but also a little relieved for her because she needed peace. She didn't deserve to finish her life like that.

She died right before I was about to go away with Aalborg for a three-week, midseason training camp. The winters in Denmark are really tough, so the soccer season takes a break from December to February, and many teams travel out to warmer countries so that they can practice in better conditions. Aalborg was holding its training camp in Miami that year, and we were scheduled to fly out just before the funeral.

I decided to go to training camp even though it meant missing the funeral. I felt like I had already said goodbye while she was still alive, and I was sure that if it had been up to her to make the same decision from upstairs, she would have told me to go. Even though life was more complicated for me by then – with adult problems like money, gambling and public image – she knew that deep down I was still just that little boy in the park, chasing soccer.

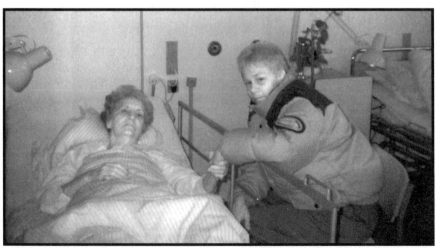

Granny was in and out of hospital a lot during the years that I knew her, but I was always sure to visit regularly. That got a little trickier during my time at Millwall, but even then I spoke to her on the phone every day.

9
CASINO JIMMY

Every day after practice at Aalborg, and sometimes before, a group of us would get together to play cards for money. The stakes were not huge – just what people could afford – but they could add up after a while. Rather than laying money out on the table, we had one guy keep score on a sheet of paper and we evened up at the end of each month.

That was just a bit of fun to keep us occupied – soccer players have a lot of free time, remember – but much more serious were the card games we had when I got called up to the Under-21 national team. There were a lot of young players on that squad who were already playing for big clubs in Europe and making a lot more money than me, so the stakes were much bigger.

It got crazy really fast. We used to play a Danish game called Mousel, and I remember one round where the numbers just kept going up and up. There were five of us in that card game but only two of us still played our soccer in Denmark; all the rest were abroad making good wages. They were making individual bets worth more than my monthly salary.

In the space of just a couple of hours, I had won $50,000 at that table, and all I could think about was what I would have done if I had lost the same amount. But it wasn't a big deal for those guys – they just got my bank details – and *Boom!* – that money was in my account within minutes. That was how it went. A few of them carried that sort of money around in their pockets. There was another occasion when we had $30,000 in hard cash sitting out on the table in a big pile, riding on one hand of cards.

I never freaked out about it, though, because thanks to all that time spent with my granny, I knew I was a pretty good card player.

That wasn't where I lost my money. If I had just played cards my whole life, I would have made a lot of money on gambling. It was the casino and the sports betting that crushed me.

Those card games became a huge deal, starting off with just a couple of us playing casually together but building up to the point that whenever there was an international game, I wouldn't be looking to see which country we were playing against, but instead, which of my gambling buddies had made the team. There were about six or seven guys who would always be up for a game of cards, and I would scan down the roster and think: *He's coming, he's coming ... yes! We have the group back together again!*

Once we got started with the cards, it became a big race to see how many games we could play. At lunch we would throw down our food and then run back to the room to start playing. We did the same thing at dinner. It was fun, but when I look back, it was also really bad. It was too much to be risking, even if I did feel like the odds were in my favor.

It wasn't the cards, though, that got me in trouble with the Danish U-21 team. If I had stayed in and just played Mousel with those guys every night while I was away on international duty, I would have never had the chance to acquire the nickname that would follow me around for the rest of my career. I would never have become 'Casino Jimmy.'

The story begins one weekend in September 1999. We had lost 3-1 to Switzerland in a U-21 European Championships qualifier on the Friday night, a result that almost certainly eliminated us from the competition. Italy was way out in front at the top of the group, and I believe that loss dropped us down into third. Even second place was not necessarily enough to reach the main tournament – you had to have a certain number of points – so it was effectively over, even though we still had one game left.

After the Switzerland defeat, we went back to our team base in Copenhagen and did a little light training for the next two days. We were supposed to fly out to Italy for our final game on Monday. Of course, we filled a lot of our dead time playing cards, but we started to get a little bored on that Sunday afternoon. I was grabbing some lunch with my friends Peter Degn and Allan Jepsen, and someone suggested that we should go to the casino nearby.

We headed there for a little while and I won a bit of money, so over dinner I was saying, "We should go back and play a little more." Our coach, Jan B Poulsen, had given the team just one rule for the evening, which was to be back in our rooms by 11:00 p.m. We agreed that we would carry on gambling at the casino until 10:30 and then catch a cab together back to the hotel.

Back we went to the casino, and this time my luck was really in. I kept hitting my numbers on the roulette wheel and was having a great time, until I looked at the clock and realized it was already 11:00 p.m. The three of us quickly got together for a team meeting. I guess I wasn't the only one doing well, because the solution we came to was to not rush back to the hotel and apologize to the coaches. Instead we said, "Well, we're already late now. How much difference does it make if it's thirty minutes or three hours?"

To be honest, we weren't really thinking about getting into trouble. We were all young, confident guys, and we thought we could probably sneak back into our rooms without being noticed. Besides, if they did catch us, what had we really done wrong? OK, we'd stayed out late, but it wasn't like we were drinking. That was the theory, anyway.

It was 2:00 in the morning by the time we left, and I had won 84,000 Danish Krone – about $15,000 – so we were in high spirits on that cab journey back to the hotel. We were a little worried that there might be a coach waiting up in the lobby when we got back, but we didn't see anyone there, so we assumed we had got away with it. Peter and Allan were rooming together, whereas I was sharing with the back-up goalkeeper, Jesper Christiansen. We said goodnight and went our separate ways.

I slipped into my room where Jesper was snoring away happily, and I got into my bed. I was just falling asleep myself when suddenly there was a knock at my door. It was about 3:00 a.m. by this point, so unless this was Allan or Peter on the other side of that door, I knew there was a good chance I was about to get into trouble. But I was still convinced the coaches couldn't have seen us because there hadn't been anyone downstairs. I quickly decided that I should just pretend I hadn't heard anything. I rolled over and closed my eyes to go back to sleep.

That was never going to work. The knocks on the door got louder and louder until it felt like the person on the other side was about to smash the whole thing down. Now Jesper was wide awake and asking me, "What's going on?" I tried telling him to go back to sleep, but it wasn't a very realistic suggestion with all that noise happening. I climbed out of bed and messed up my hair to make it look like I had been sleeping. I opened the door, squinting as though I had just woken up. Of course, it was Coach Poulsen standing on the other side.

"What are you doing coach? I'm tired."

"Stop acting stupid. I know you only just got back to the hotel."

"What do you mean? I've been asleep for hours."

"Don't be stupid, you little shit. I know you've been out and I know you've been up to something, so you better tell me the truth or things will only be worse for you."

I tried to argue for a few more seconds, but it was clear that he knew exactly when we'd returned. I found out how in the newspapers a few days later. It had been the birthday of one of the coaches, so they were all in the hotel bar having a quiet drink to celebrate. That was right by the lobby, meaning they got to see all the other players come back in. Coach Poulsen still hadn't seen us by the time he went to bed, so he gave the receptionist instructions to phone up to his room as soon as we arrived. The receptionist did as he was told, and now Coach Paulsen was at my door.

Finally I caved, saying, "OK coach, I'm sorry. The truth is that I've been out at a casino. I lost track of time, but I promise you I haven't been drinking or anything like that. I just didn't realize how late it was."

"Thank you," he replied. "Thank you for actually telling me the truth... unlike these two."

I hadn't even mentioned Allan or Peter, but now he opened up the door fully and there they were, standing in the corridor next to him. They had told him a completely different story, saying we had been playing cards up in another room. I felt awful. I had shown them up as liars, but not on purpose. If we had spoken about it beforehand, we could all have given him the same story, but because we thought nobody saw us coming back in, we never even thought about it.

Coach Poulsen told us we would be suspended for the Italy game and that we should go back to bed. The first part of that verdict I accepted – that was his prerogative. But if that was the decision, then there was no way I was waiting around in that hotel until morning just to be made an example of. I replied, "If I'm suspended, then I'm going to leave right now."

"You can't leave right now," he said. "It's the middle of the night. Go back to bed and we will talk about this in the morning."

"No. If I'm suspended, then I will leave."

Eventually he went and woke up the rest of the staff, and we had to wait in another room while they talked about the decision. When he came back, he confirmed the suspension.

My manager at Aalborg at that time was Hans Backe, the man who would go on to coach the New York Red Bulls for three seasons, from 2010 to 2012. He was a tough, aggressive guy who did not tolerate bad behavior from his players. All I could think the whole time I waited for Coach Poulsen and his assistants to make their decision was that I needed to explain the situation to Backe before anyone else did.

I called my dad and told him everything. He agreed with me and said, "Get home as soon as possible." He wasn't really angry at me, maybe because he could hear how scared I already was.

Allan and Peter decided to come with me, and we got the receptionist – the same guy who told the coach when we came in – to call us a taxi. Copenhagen to Aalborg is a four-hour drive, and we didn't even take the most direct route because both Peter and Allan lived in different places and we had to drop them off on the way. That cab ride cost – and I'm not exaggerating here – $2,000. Good thing I'd had such a successful night at the casino!

I had the taxi drop me off at home. I changed clothes and drove as fast as I could down to Aalborg's training facility. I pulled into the parking lot just as the assistant manager was getting out of his car. He greeted me with a big smile.

"Hey Jimmy! How are you? Aren't you supposed to be in Italy right now?"

"Something bad has happened. Can we go talk about it with Coach Backe in his office?"

He must have seen the look on my face because we went straight up there. I was so afraid of Hans Backe at that time. He is one of the best coaches I have worked with in my entire career – extremely smart and an excellent teacher – but he was a total hard-ass. I went in there expecting him to rip my head off. But I had no choice: it was either this way or wait for him to find out via the newspapers. So I got into that office and told him everything. He sat there listening, not giving anything away. When I was finished, he asked me one question: "Was there any alcohol involved?"

"Absolutely not," I said.

"Then you've got my full support, 100%."

While I had been driving to the facility, the Danish Soccer Federation put out a press release detailing our suspensions, and as I stood there in Backe's office I could see the media cars and vans pulling into the parking lot. Neither of the other two guys played in Denmark at that time – Allan was with Heerenveen in Holland, while Peter was at Everton – so all of the media focus landed on me.

Later that morning, I went out to take part in practice as usual. The team's general manager told me not to speak to any reporters until the press conference they had scheduled for the afternoon. That turned out to be a crazy scene, the room so packed with reporters that you had people outside the doors, fighting to get in. I think it was the busiest media day in the club's history. But Coach Backe stuck up for me just like he said he would. I was so grateful for the way he treated me.

The next few days were ridiculous in the papers. I was getting crushed, and not just by the reporters. They interviewed a bunch of guys from the senior national team who started talking about how unprofessional our behavior was.

Then, the following weekend, Aalborg was playing on the road against Lyngby, and that's where my new nickname started. The Lyngby fans were chanting "Casino Jimmy! Casino Jimmy!" They threw some other chants out there, too. They were actually pretty creative, and I found some of it quite funny.

From that day on, the nickname followed me everywhere. Any time my name was mentioned in the newspaper, they wouldn't write "Jimmy Nielsen" but instead "Casino Jimmy" – whether I had a good game or a bad one. It would just say, "Casino Jimmy made a great save in the 35th minute" or "Casino Jimmy cost his team with a terrible mistake."

It didn't really bother me, but after a few years I got to the point where I was a little bored of hearing it. After one game, somebody asked me yet another question about it and I said, "It doesn't bother me, but I don't think it's that funny anymore. It's kind of an old story." Of course, the next day the headline read: "Jimmy Nielsen is furious at the media for calling him Casino Jimmy." And then it got even funnier for everyone else to call me that name again. I really didn't mind, though. I can promise you that I've been called much worse things on the soccer field.

The nickname that many fans in the US know me by is 'White Puma,' which also started around the same time. That was a much less exciting story. We were having a shooting session at Aalborg and I was flying around, making saves and obviously having a good day. One of the guys shouted, "You look like a white puma." It stuck. So it's always one of those two nicknames: I'm either Casino Jimmy or the White Puma.

People often ask me if that night at the casino is the biggest regret of my soccer career. Not really. I didn't kill anyone, I didn't drive drunk, and I didn't cheat anybody. I broke a rule, I came home late, and I got punished for it. The U-21 team lost that next game without me, but we were not going to qualify anyway at that point. Plus, that Italy team did not lose a single game in qualifying and went on to win the whole tournament, so even if I had played, there is no guarantee that the game would have gone any differently. In the end, the person I hurt most was me.

I'm not saying what I did was right, but it was not the end of the world. I also think that if Coach Poulsen really wanted to punish me, he should have taken me to Italy and made me sit on the bench. That would have been much worse for me personally, and it could have avoided making such a big deal in the media. In my opinion, he overreacted.

That was Coach Poulsen's last game with Danish U-21 team before he took a job with the Singapore national soccer team. I was suspended for just the one game, against Italy, after which I went straight back into the team under the new coach. Unfortunately, the next game was the exhibition against England, where I let in four goals while trying to impress Alex Ferguson. After that I was too old to play for the U-21.

I never got to play for the senior national team. Although I was called up ten or twelve times over the course of my career, I always wound up being the back-up to Peter Schmeichel or later to Thomas Sørensen, another really great goalkeeper, who has spent most of his career in the Premier League. It was amazing to watch Schmeichel in training those few times. He was like a wall in front of his goal, saving everything. But I got the impression the team was a bit scared of him as well. Because he was so good, he had an aura about him which made it hard to treat him like a normal person.

Does it make me sad that I didn't get to do more with Denmark? I'm not sure if I would go that far. I'm not someone who really harbours regrets, but certainly when I was younger I had hoped and expected to do more with the national team in my career.

Like everyone else in the country, I remember watching us win the European Championships in 1992 and how incredible that felt. Ask almost anyone in Denmark and they will tell you exactly where they were and what they were doing on the day of the final, when we beat Germany 2-0. As a fifteen-year-old kid dreaming of a career in soccer at the time, it was one of those events that left a big impression on me.

I had been at my dad's bookie during the day, and it was extremely busy in there with people placing their bets for the final. One of the guys who worked there was so certain that Denmark wasn't going to win that he offered me odds of 5-1. I bet 200 krone (about $35) with him. Then I cycled over from there to watch the final with my family at one of my dad's nightclubs. It was completely packed with people, and it was the most excited I have ever been to watch a game of soccer.

Even in Denmark, nobody gave us a chance of winning that game, but John Jensen scored after about 20 minutes and then Schmeichel started making all of these great saves. Denmark got a second goal with about 10 minutes to go and the place just went absolutely crazy.

That was how it finished, 2-0. Afterward I was cycling home (via the bookie to collect my money) and there were people hanging out of windows on every street, waving the Danish flag. Every car that went by was honking its horn, and the drivers were leaning out of the windows and cheering.

When I eventually got called up to the Danish U-17 team, the soccer federation sent me a letter with various bits and pieces of information. On the outside of the envelope was a message proclaiming: "We Are The Champions!" That was very inspiring. It made me want to go out and win something for the country, just like the 1992 team had done.

And I did care about my country. The only time in my whole career that I remember feeling nervous before a game of soccer was with the U-17 team. It was a European Championships qualifier against Portugal, which we needed to win to reach the main tournament. I don't know if it was because Denmark had won the senior tournament, but I was desperate for us to get through. I had butterflies in my stomach all morning before the game.

Sadly, we lost 1-0 to a goal from Maniche, another player who went on to have a pretty impressive career with Porto, Chelsea and Atlético Madrid. I had just saved a shot before their goal, but he came in to score the rebound.

I don't know if that trip to the casino cost me the chance to play more for the senior team later down the line. Certainly I got the impression that the coach, Morten Olsen, didn't really like me. Before I was ever called up for the senior team, I told one of the big sports magazines in Denmark, *Tipsbladet*, that even if every other Danish goalkeeper was on a plane that crashed, Morten Olsen would find somebody else rather than pick me. Two weeks later, he called me up for the first time. They made fun of me at the team dinner for what I'd told the newspaper.

He still never put me in the team though, and I've wondered plenty of times how things might have been different if the previous coach, Bo Johansen, had stayed around. He was only in the job until 2000, but he started me a few times for the *Ligalandsholdet*, a separate national team run by the same manager but which only uses players from the Danish league, rather than players whose careers have taken them abroad.

In the end, it doesn't really matter. Everyone makes mistakes in their lives, and I certainly made one that night at the casino. The important thing is that you learn from those mistakes. Unfortunately, at least in the short term, I didn't.

If you needed proof of how the Casino Jimmy nickname stuck with me, here it is. This article, in a newspaper called Aalborg Stiftstidende, was published several years after I got in trouble for missing curfew with the Denmark Under-21 team and does not even mention gambling, but the photographer still had me pose in front of a casino anyway. As I've said many times, the nickname really doesn't bother me. I've been called much worse on a soccer field.

10
JANNIE

There is one very important person who I have not told you about yet. Jannie, my wife, came into my life when I was still just thirteen years old, and I can honestly say I have no idea where I would be today if she hadn't. She is an unbelievable woman, the love of my life, and I hope that over the course of this book, I will have a few opportunities to show how much she means to me. The only reason I had not mentioned her before this point is because I knew she would tell the story of how we got together much better than I would. So for now, it's over to her!

Jimmy is right that I love telling this story. I'm one year older than him, so I was fourteen when we first met, and you won't be surprised to hear that he was playing soccer at the time. It was during the period when he was playing for Norwich, and the team used to travel over to Denmark regularly for tournaments and practice sessions in a small town called Nørhalne. That was where he played for Norwich for the very first time, when their goalkeeper got sick.

I lived in Aalborg, too, at that age, but I had a good friend in Nørhalne who I used to visit every weekend. We were getting interested in boys, and we liked to go and look at them while they played soccer in the park. The second I saw Jimmy, I thought he was fantastic. Not at soccer – I never cared about that at all – but just to look at! He was not nearly as big as he is now, but I was pretty small at that age, and to me he looked very tall, with these big broad shoulders. He had blonde hair that he wore long at the back, like someone from Sweden!

I thought he was the best thing ever. The first couple of times we went to the games, I only watched him from the sideline, but eventually

I plucked up the courage to go and say hello. I don't really remember that first conversation at all now, only that we were both a little shy. But I went home that evening and told my mom: "Today I met the guy I'm going to marry one day." I'm sure she didn't believe me.

Unfortunately, Jimmy already had a girlfriend at that time. I wasn't happy about that because I wanted to be his girlfriend, but instead of pushing myself on him, I started becoming friends with his friends. I don't know if that was me being smart or not, but it did mean that I would get invited to any parties he was going to. I think some of his friends liked me, but I only went so I could look at Jimmy.

Although we weren't going out straight away, we did have some things in common. I used to sing at that age, and it was pretty serious. My father had a record label and had suggested when I was about eight that I should record some kids' songs. They did very well, and after that I started doing shows every weekend in theaters, halls, and on national TV.

It meant that I usually had to leave those parties early because I was going to be up early the next day. Jimmy had the same thing with soccer. Our moms would always be the first ones to come pick us up, and I think we both appreciated having someone else who was in the same situation and who understood why you would make those decisions. That said, I stopped singing at fifteen; unlike Jimmy with his soccer.

We didn't just see each other at parties, though. My father loved horse racing, and he decided at a certain point to invest in part-ownership of a few horses. Jimmy's dad, separately, did the same thing, and somewhere down the line they started talking to one another about it. They became friends, and sometimes my dad would go look at horses together with Jimmy's dad at the stables. I would tag along, hoping Jimmy might be there. I didn't actually care about the horses any more than I cared about the soccer, though, so if Jimmy wasn't there, it would be a very long day!

It was only a few years later that Jimmy and I realized we had been going to the same horse racing track ever since we were really little. The difference was that when I was six or seven years old, I would just run off to the playground with the other kids. Jimmy stayed watching the races, which is why we never met sooner.

When I was around sixteen, my family moved to Blokhus, a very small town by the beach, about 45 minutes outside of Aalborg. At that point, Jimmy and I were seeing each other a little less, but one day I came home and my mom told me he had called to say hi. I didn't believe her at first because he didn't usually call, but she was sure it was him. I felt too shy to call back, so I decided to write him a postcard instead. It had a picture of a pig on the front, pointing its nose at the camera. I know exactly what it looked like because Jimmy never threw it away – he still has it today!

He nearly didn't get it, though, because I gave it to my mom to send and she completely forgot. A few days later, I was looking for something in her purse and saw that the card was still in there. I took it out and sent it myself, but I still wonder how different life might have been if I had never noticed.

Just a few days after I sent it, Jimmy gave me a call and, after a fun conversation, asked me to come and see him that Saturday. He was single by then, and we had a great night together. That was where it all started.

I would like to say we were together forever after that, but it's not quite true. We were on-and-off for a little while, and not long after my 18th birthday, I moved even farther away to a city called Odense. That was more than two hours' drive away, which doesn't sound like a lot in America, but in Denmark, that's a big deal! I had a job there as a waitress, which is something I always wanted to do. I knew I wouldn't want to do it after I had kids, so this was the chance to do it while I was still young.

Jimmy and I were not really in a relationship at this point, but we would go visit each other and have dates from time to time. And maybe we weren't as careful as we should have been, because at twenty-one, I became pregnant. I told Jimmy, and he was a little surprised, but he took it incredibly well. I left my job and moved back to live with my parents at first because I knew they could help me with the baby.

I was scared because I had never even held a baby before. But from the moment Jimmy first set eyes on our little girl, Mille, I knew he was going to do great. It was March when I gave birth, and it was freezing cold outside, so Jimmy came in wearing his jacket still covered in snow. As soon as he walked into the room, he had his arms out, saying: "Oh my God, can I hold her?" The way he took it in stride made me feel like everything was going to be alright.

That is one of the things I love most about Jimmy: he is always so calm, he never loses his head. Well, maybe he does on the soccer field, but he leaves it all out there. When he comes home after a game, no matter what the result, he does something very similar to what he did that day, walking in the front door and saying, "Girls, come on over." We have one more daughter now, Isabella, and we will run over to give Jimmy a hug. His being like that makes me feel calmer as well.

Now that I was back in Aalborg and we had Mille together, he was round at my parents' house all the time. After three months, we decided that we were ready to take the next step, so we moved in together in the summer of 1998.

We didn't get married for another three years, and a big part of that was because of his gambling. I knew from the moment I met Jimmy that soccer was his number one priority, and I never expected to change that. When I agreed to move in with him, I told myself that as long as I was the next-most important thing after soccer, then I would be happy. But the gambling? I never signed up for that.

It would be years before I knew quite how bad his problems were, but the longer we were together, the more I would see. Jimmy was a different guy when he was gambling, and he would disappear into another world where you couldn't reach him. Sometimes he would physically disappear for hours or even days at a time and I wouldn't know where he was. He never let me know the sums he was betting, but I knew his behavior wasn't right.

The first two times he proposed to me, I said no, and both times it was because of the gambling. They were big, romantic proposals, too. The first time he had cooked me a beautiful dinner at home (and he doesn't cook very often!), and the second time, he took me out to dinner and a fancy hotel with the bed covered in flower petals.

After all that, I finally said yes the third time around, after he proposed to me in the car one day when we were doing nothing special at all. I didn't really believe he had changed, but I also knew that despite everything, we wanted to be together. I suppose I also knew that after a certain point he probably wouldn't keep on asking! It was the right decision in the end, even if we did have some tough times ahead. I would do it all again to be where we are today.

The wedding was very small. It was the fall of 2001 when Jimmy proposed that third time, and we talked for a while about doing something big the following summer. But the more we talked, the bigger it got and in the end we realized that getting married shouldn't be about everybody else, it should be about what we wanted. So we booked a date at the city hall for that same December. We invited nobody except Mille and a friend of mine who was going to serve as a witness.

We didn't tell anybody, not even our parents, but the one problem we had was that the date was on a Tuesday, and Jimmy was supposed to be at practice. He went to speak to the general manager, Lynge, who I think he's told you a little bit about already. Jimmy asked if he could have the day off, but Lynge wasn't going to say yes until he got a good reason. Finally, Jimmy told him about the wedding, but he begged him not to say anything to anyone else because we really didn't want it to be a big deal.

On the day of the wedding, we went to the city hall and had our little ceremony, just me, Jimmy, Mille and my friend. We had booked a table for lunch afterwards, but as we were coming down the steps, we saw Lynge. He had not told a soul, but he came along himself and was waiting with a bottle of champagne for us and a glass of Coke for Mille. That was very sweet.

We went for lunch afterwards, and the next day Jimmy went back to practice. That was perfect for us. And Jimmy was perfect for me, even if there were times over the next few years when it wouldn't always feel like it.

Now that Jannie has told you the nice part, it is my duty to tell you the stuff I'm less proud of. You can see from all those proposals how much I wanted her to marry me, and I wouldn't have been like that if I wasn't crazy in love with her. Unfortunately, that still did not stop me from letting her down badly on lots of occasions in the years that followed.

One of the worst instances occurred on a vacation we took to the United States. We were still in our early twenties, so it was the first time we had really been away together. It was at the end of the season, so I had time off. Jannie's parents agreed to look after Mille while we went away. We booked five days in Los Angeles and then a couple of nights in Las Vegas to round off the trip. You can probably guess where things started to go wrong.

L.A. was great. We saw the tourist sights and Jannie got to do some good shopping, but the whole time I was there all I could think about was getting to Vegas and placing some bets. I had seen it in films and on TV, and for a hardcore gambler like me, it felt like the Promised Land. The casinos in Denmark are only small, with a handful of tables operating at any given time, but in Vegas, I imagined enormous rooms full of roulette tables and card games.

It more than lived up to my expectations. We were staying at the Treasure Island resort, and from the moment I first walked out onto the casino floor, I just remember feeling this huge buzz from being surrounded by so much fast money.

Jannie wasn't that interested in gambling, so she went to have a look at the shops while I hit the tables. For the first few hours I was killing it, winning a lot of money. After a while, Jannie came back to the hotel to take a nap, but I stayed down there at the roulette table. My numbers kept coming up. I had won about $20,000 by dinnertime, and I got my chips changed into big handfuls of twenties and fifties. I went up to the room and woke Jannie up to show her my winnings. We just started dancing around the room, throwing the money up in the air and jumping on the bed.

We went to dinner and I gave her some money to go shopping again. I went back to the tables. Eventually she came back and said she was going to bed, but I stayed down there to carry on gambling. My luck had turned, and by this point I had lost most of what I won earlier in the day. But I had come to Vegas prepared – I had a secret stash of extra gambling money tucked into the inside pocket of my jacket, about $30,000 in Danish currency that Jannie didn't know about.

Soon that money was gone, too. With nothing left, I had no choice but to go back up to my room and crawl into bed. I slept for maybe an hour. After that I was just lying in bed, staring at the ceiling and thinking about getting back to the casino to win back what I had lost. I knew we had a few thousand dollars of emergency money in the safety deposit box, so I nudged Jannie awake and asked her for the combination. She gave it to me and straight away I climbed out of bed and took the money with me back down to the casino floor.

Of course, I lost that money, too. When I came back up to the room, Jannie was wide awake and looking panicked. "Where the hell have you been?" she asked.

"I went down to have a gamble."

"But the safety deposit box is open!"

"Yeah, you gave me the combination so that I could get the money out."

"No I didn't. I haven't spoken to you since I went to bed."

She had given me the number in her sleep. After that we were up for a few hours talking about what had happened. She had seen all that money I won earlier in the day, so even though she didn't know about my secret stash, she knew I must have lost a lot of money. I was pretty unpopular that night, but I'm sorry to say that wasn't the lowest point of the trip.

Jannie lent me her credit card the next day so I could have some spending money, but I took it and went gambling again. I lost a ton of money on her card, which she was furious about, and on the last day I tried to borrow even more off her. This time she said no, but I kept asking over and over, telling her I only needed a little bit and would pay her back when we got home. She got so desperate that she wound up locking herself in our bathroom just to get away. Even then, I stood outside for a while, telling her to pass me the card underneath the door.

Already, at twenty years old, I was sick in my head for gambling. I honestly can't tell you what was going through my mind as I stood outside that bathroom door, beyond the simple thought that I needed to get some money to bet with so I could win back the money I had lost. As a serious gambler you were always doing that, chasing your losses, but by doing that, you only make them bigger. Then you have to bet even more to turn it around, and it just keeps on getting worse.

Eventually I calmed down and Jannie came out of the bathroom. Again, we had a long conversation and she said that I had a problem. I told her I agreed with her, but inside I didn't really believe it. Certainly I wasn't in any great rush to change, because about a year later we had another vacation together where I let things get similarly out of hand.

This time, we were on a Mediterranean cruise. We stopped at various ports along the way, one of which was Monaco, another city known for its casinos. When the ship stopped there, I hopped off and went straight to a casino, handed my card to the cashier and asked for some chips. But the guy behind the counter had one look at my card, took off his glasses said, "Only gold cards accepted."

I couldn't believe it. I stood there thinking, *I'm in Monaco and I can't gamble – this is a disaster*, but then an English guy I had met on the cruise came up behind me and asked what was happening. He offered to lend me a bit of money for some chips, which I happily took, but I wasn't going to ask someone I barely knew for a huge amount, so it was only a hundred bucks or so. As usual, I lost it, but I paid him back once we were on the boat.

The real gambling happened on the ship itself. There was a casino on board, but that particular cruise worked on a payment system where you never handed over cash for anything. They just gave you a plastic card when you got on board, and every time you bought something you charged it to the card before settling up at the end of the trip.

So every night I headed down to the ship's casino, threw down the plastic card and said, "I need $1,000 worth of chips." Maybe a bit more than that, depending on how I felt. But I never handed over any actual money, so I wasn't keeping track of how much I really spent. Every night I could just go down there, give them the card and spend some more money without really thinking about it.

On the last morning, I woke up to see that a letter had been slipped underneath the door of our cabin. The manager of the cruise wanted to speak to me urgently. They had been trying to charge my card for the amount I spent, but it got rejected because I didn't have that much in my account. Not for the last time, Jannie had to bail me out.

Throwing away money was not the only way I let her down. In my early twenties, I started investing in a few racehorses, buying shares in them together with different friends and family. Jannie's family, as she has explained, loved their horses too, so one of the first ones I got was jointly owned between me, my dad, my brother, Jannie's dad and her brother.

On December 11th, 2002, that horse had a big race in Sweden, where the prize money for racing is much better than in Denmark. We all agreed to go and watch it run. Normally I wouldn't remember the exact date of a race that long ago, but there's a good reason why I can on this occasion. December 11th was the day Jannie and I got married. The race was taking place on our first wedding anniversary.

Jannie didn't say anything at first, but the day before I was supposed to go, she asked me, "Do you know what day it is tomorrow?" At that point the penny really should have dropped, but I said, "No." She had to tell me that it was our anniversary. I apologized to her over and over and promised that, even though I was still going to go, I could make it good. I went out to the shops thinking I would buy her something really special as a way of apologizing.

Instead, I bought her an alarm clock. It was the worst gift *ever*, because not only was it completely unromantic, it was also something that she absolutely didn't need. Jannie is one of those people who wake-up early every morning on their own; she had no use for such a thing. But I had been searching through the store when I found this clock that had a button which projected the time onto the ceiling. In that moment, I thought it was awesome.

So I bought the clock and went to buy myself a suit for the trip to Sweden. I was good friends with the guy who ran the clothing store, and he asked me what I had in the bag. I told him it was an anniversary gift for my wife. He asked me what I got her. I should have known from his reaction that this wasn't a good idea. "Oh my God, you have to be joking," he said. "You can't buy her an alarm clock for your anniversary."

I was confident, though, and I told him she would love it. I was wrong. Jannie didn't get angry or tell me off, but the second I gave it to her I could see how disappointed she was. The worst bit was that she had put in a really big effort for my gift, ordering a special money clip from America, gold and in the shape of a dollar sign. I loved it. It was the perfect thing for me at that age, and I still keep it in my wallet today.

Looking back on it now, we both see the funny side – that alarm clock was so ridiculous! But the truth is that she deserved a big trophy and a medal for staying with me after the way I had behaved. Even by this stage, I still had a long way to fall.

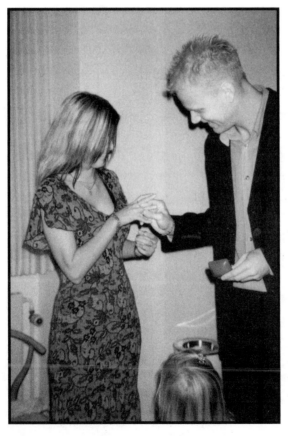

As Jannie explains in this chapter, our wedding was a low-key affair. I'm putting the ring on her finger in this photo, and 50% of our congregation is in the shot – since you can see the back of our daughter Mille's head. I have lots of great friends, but I've never liked hosting big parties that are all about me. Jannie is the same way, so this was perfect for both of us.

My first day at school. I don't remember it at all. And I don't remember much of what they taught me over the next 10 years either! I spent most of my time in class thinking about my next game of soccer.

Here I am getting ready for a game with the Aalborg Under-5 team. That's me on the near end of the line with the green goalkeeper's jersey. Whatever happened to all that hair? I think I must have lost it all gambling.

Granny was pretty sick for the last few years of her life, but she had a great spirit and kept on smiling, even when she was in a lot of pain. This photo looks like it was taken on her birthday. That's me behind her, with my brother Johnny seated on the edge of the chair.

An early team photo from my days with B52. I'm crouched down in the front row on the right-hand side, and my best buddy Mikkel is standing on the same end of the back row, next to one of our coaches.

Here's another shot of me playing with B52, collecting a runners-up trophy at the end of a tournament. I remember that game because it finished with a penalty shoot-out, and even though I was the goalkeeper, I wound up taking one. I scored it, but we still lost.

At the age of 17, I was already living on my own in London and backing up Kasey Keller for Millwall. I found time to be a tourist some days, too – getting photos like this one of me with a big red London bus.

Millwall was paying me thousands of dollars per week to play soccer, but I still had to scrub my own boots clean at the end of every practice session. I had it better than the academy players, though. I was the same age as those guys and a lot of them had to scrub the veteran players' boots, as well as their own.

My mom and dad ran bars and nightclubs together for a long time, and once I started playing for Aalborg, they used me to help drum up a little bit of local publicity. That's them next to me in the picture, and I'm pretty sure this is opening night for a new bar they had just launched. I don't normally go to the bar in my goalie's uniform!

This is me in action for Aalborg. I love that goalkeeping jersey – there's a lot going on with all those colors – but the most important thing about this photo is that I kept the ball out of the net. If I remember correctly, it was a close-range header from a corner, and I made the save.

101

Sporting Kansas City holds preseason training camp sometimes down in Orlando, but this photo was actually taken at the Disneyland in Paris in about 2007. I don't really like theme parks – they're too crowded for me – but the girls had a good time meeting Mickey Mouse.

Photo courtesy of AP Images

Opening day at Sporting Park. That was a fantastic occasion, extremely exciting with fireworks going off and planes flying overhead before kickoff. We have fireworks on the field before a lot of our home games. Even when I know they're coming, they still make me jump out of my skin. They're so loud!

102

Photo courtesy of Kory Brinton

How cool is this view? When I walked out of the tunnel for our US Open Cup final against Seattle, the first thing I saw was three huge rainbows over Sporting Park. You can only really see two of them here, but it's still an awesome shot.

Photo courtesy of Kory Brinton

I pulled out all the stops before Eddie Johnson's penalty in the US Open Cup final: doing everything I could to distract him. I actually get embarrassed when I look at photos like this one now; what sort of psycho does stuff like that? But I was just trying to make the whole situation as unusual for him as I could – to take him out of his comfort zone. And it worked, because he missed his PK. I would have pulled my pants down if that was what it took to win that final.

Photo courtesy of Gary Rohman

We are the champions! As a goalkeeper you get used to celebrating on your own, because usually when something good happens, it's at the other end of the field. So when Eddie Johnson missed his penalty, it was actually a little awkward as I didn't really know what to do. All my teammates had been watching from the halfway line, so I just started running toward them as they were running back toward me. Winning that trophy might just be the greatest moment of my career.

Photo courtesy of Jamila St. Ann

As I ran toward my teammates at the end of the US Open Cup final, I slid down onto my knees in celebration. But as soon as I did, I realized what a terrible mistake I'd made. If I stayed down there, everybody would jump on top and I would get crushed. So at the second when this photo was taken, all I'm thinking is: I've got to get back up! Thankfully I managed it, just in time.

Photo courtesy of Kory Brinton

Here I am standing on the podium with my US Open Cup winners' medal and, of course, my tongue sticking out. I actually have no idea where that medal is now. I've never worried too much about physical mementos. The memories are what matter to me.

Photo courtesy of Jamila St. Ann

What a feeling it was to finally get our hands on the US Open Cup. I have not won as much as I would have liked in my career, but moments like this keep me coming back for more. When it's cold and raining at practice and I'm feeling too exhausted to train, I just remember how amazing it felt to be out there celebrating with my teammates.

Photo courtesy of Gary Rohman

As you can see, we had a fun party in the locker room after the US Open Cup win. I can't tell you exactly what's going on in this photo, but that's Kei Kamara up on the table and he's just poured half a bottle of champagne over my head. I'm not a big drinker at all, and I didn't stay out late like the younger members of the team, but I did have one or two beers there in the locker room. Put it this way: I had enough that I didn't drive myself home afterward!

Photo courtesy of Kory Brinton

Upper 90 Photography

Right after the US Open Cup final and after we had showered and changed back into our regular clothes, we were allowed to bring our families in to get a picture with the trophy. This is one of my all-time favorite photos, and I have it hanging up on a wall at home.

Along with the rest of Sporting Kansas City's players, I had the great honor of being invited to Kauffman Stadium to show off the US Open Cup trophy before a Royals game. Kei Kamara did the ceremonial opening pitch, and I stood behind the plate as the catcher. He nailed the pitch and I made the catch. My family came along to watch, too, because they love baseball. I don't mind it, but I usually get bored and want to go home after about five innings. Jannie and the girls always want to stay to the end.

This is what you call a leaning tower of Nielsens. We are on vacation in the Cayman Islands, taking a little dip in the ocean. We actually wanted Jannie to join in as well and make it a four-person tower, but she was worried that someone would fall down and hurt themselves.

I still like to play cards with my daughters like I used to do growing up with my granny, but unlike back then we never play for money. Instead, I make them play for push-ups. And I'm a pretty good card player, so they usually wind up having to do quite a few! We always end up fighting, though, because we're all such bad losers. The girls definitely got that trait from their dad.

Kansas City is far too hot in the summer, but at least it gives us an excuse to jump in the pool. In Denmark, if anybody had a pool, all they'd be able to use it for is ice skating.

Looks like I lassoed me a wife! Jannie and I were invited to attend a Garth Brooks concert in 2012, which served as a fundraiser for his charity, Teammates For Kids. It's a great charity, and for every dollar we put in at the event, Garth would triple it. This photo is just us goofing around before the concert, but if you've seen the picture at the front of this book, then you already know I make a pretty good cowboy.

"Jimmy Nielsen Rocks," reads the sign on the videoboard in this picture. I actually have that sign at home. It was made by some girls who go to school with my daughter Mille.

Photo courtesy of AP Images

I have had many things thrown at me on a soccer field before now, but the bobblehead which hit me in the eye during our game against Portland in August 2011 was definitely a new one! I had a few stitches put in so I could finish the game, but my eye had swollen up so much by full-time that I could barely see out of it.

Photo courtesy of Gary Rohman

Here I am at Sporting Kansas City's home opener for 2013. Jannie loves the new black goalie's uniform – she thinks it makes me look tough!

112

11
CHAMPIONS OF DENMARK

Aalborg won its first-ever league title the year before I arrived. There was always pressure on us players to do it again after that, to deliver more trophies, but I didn't mind at all. I still thought I would be sold before too long, but if I was going to be around for any length of time, then of course I wanted to win things.

My first three seasons were frustrating. We had a good team and were usually in the top half of the table, but we were never quite in the title race. The manager who had led Aalborg to that first championship, Poul Erik Andreasen, left immediately after doing so, and he was replaced by Sepp Piontek, the guy who didn't know my name when he introduced me to the reporters. We went through another two managers over the next couple of years, and it's always hard to get things right when you have instability at the top.

Hans Backe got the job in 1998 and things changed immediately. He didn't always treat his players well, but he was an excellent coach. His practices were extremely well-prepared, and everything we did had a purpose. You knew he had spent a lot of time studying every opponent and finding their weaknesses, so if you were working on a new drill during practice it was usually because he had seen something he thought we could exploit.

He was also lucky to be around at a time when the club was doing very well financially, which allowed him to sign some great players right away. Backe brought in a few Swedish guys – he's from Sweden himself – but his best piece of business was getting Norwegian midfielder Ståle Solbakken to join us from Wimbledon. Ståle was one of those players who just read the game perfectly and knew how to play the little short passes that don't necessarily look great on TV but create opportunities which nobody else on the field would have seen.

Ståle was about thirty and had already played a lot of games for Norway, so Backe made him our captain right away. That was a good choice because not only was he the best player on the team, he was also a good leader and well-liked in the locker room. Since retiring, Ståle has gone on to be a fairly successful manager with FC Copenhagen, FC Koln, and Wolverhampton Wanderers. I think he probably had a little bit of the coach in him when he was still playing.

It was important to have someone like Ståle bridging the gap to the manager, because as much as we respected Hans Backe, there were a lot of players who didn't like him. He wasn't very good at relating to people or dealing with different personalities, and because the club had all that money at the time, he didn't even have to make an effort. If someone annoyed Backe, he would simply go out and buy a replacement.

One way or another, the formula worked during his first season in charge. We had a great year, playing some fantastic, attractive soccer, and with three games left on the schedule, we were top of the league by two points. We had a home game against B-93 (not the team I used to play for as a kid, though the name is similar), who were bottom of the league and who we had beaten 5-1 away from home earlier that season. A win would put us within touching distance of Aalborg's second-ever title.

You would think that the crowd should be right behind us. Instead, within just a few minutes of kick-off, they started to boo. I was shocked. We had lost in the Danish Cup final about ten days earlier, so perhaps they were nervous that the whole season was about to collapse. But even if that was true, then it certainly wouldn't help our chances to have them booing us now. We hadn't done anything wrong in that game against B-93, either. Maybe we weren't playing as well as we had earlier in the season, but we had a lot of possession and I don't remember having to make any big saves. We won 2-0, but even after we took the lead, the fans continued to jeer us.

It was always like that at Aalborg: such passionate fans, but so angry when things were not going exactly how they wanted it. There was another cup final that we lost a few years later, at the end of which we walked over to thank our supporters – 15,000 of them had made the trip from Aalborg to Copenhagen to see the game. We were all waving and applauding, and our captain at that time, Jens Jessen, decided to throw them his jersey. He turned to walk away, but two seconds later he felt something hit him in the back of his head. It was his jersey; the fan who caught it was so disgusted with our performance that he threw it straight back.

We had a few heartbreaks in the cup. Aalborg reached the final three times while I was there and lost every time: 2-1 to Akademisk in 1999, 1-0 to Viborg in 2000, then 1-0 again to FC Copenhagen in 2004. That was no fun, though I've always found it worse to lose in the semifinals than in the final itself. The few times we lost in the semis were especially disappointing because we didn't even get to be part of the big game.

Anyway, getting back to our title challenge, we beat B-93 the same day that Brondby, the team in second place, lost 1-0 to FC Copenhagen. Now we were five points clear with just two games left. You always try not to look past the next game, but in the back of your mind you thought, *Surely we can't blow it from here.* We had a two-week break before the next game, at home to Lyngby. They were fourth in the table, a pretty good team.

I was sick the whole week leading up to that game against Lyngby, not with nerves, but with the flu. I had a ridiculously high temperature and couldn't get out of bed. It was terrible. I didn't practice all week, and I still had a fever when I woke up on the morning of the game. After working so hard to reach this point, I was not willing to miss the day we might win the title. I called up the team doctor and started telling him, "I'm feeling fine, no problem, I'm going to play."

The doctor understood the situation. He said, "Well, you know I'm not going to let you play if you have a temperature, so if I were you, I definitely wouldn't take any medicine that might keep the fever down." His tone made it clear that he was inviting me to read between the lines. I said, "No, no, no, doctor, of course not," then went to find some medicine that would do just that. Your normal body temperature is 98.6 degrees Fahrenheit, and when they took mine before the game, it was maybe 99 degrees. I was very grateful to the doctor for that advice.

That was an amazing day. The sun was shining and the stadium was packed, and as we came out onto the field, the fans started throwing red and white (Aalborg's uniform colors) confetti up into the air. This time they were firmly behind us, even though the match was a lot less straightforward. We scored pretty early to go up 1-0, and we led 2-1 at halftime. But in the second half, Lyngby came back and got in front at 3-2. I was completely to blame for their third goal.

It was what I would call a 'Tim Flowers moment' because it was identical to a really famous mistake made by the English goalkeeper of that name during a game between Blackburn Rovers and Liverpool a few years earlier. I'd dug a little hole in the turf just in front of my goal during the second half so that I could use the extra mud to build a tee for my goal-kicks. But then this shot came in from one of their forwards, and it hit that tee before skipping right over my head into the net.

I was so mad at myself, but our team had a great mentality that year. Any time we had a setback like that, we would say, "OK, let's go get another goal, then."

There was a really famous game about a month earlier where something very similar had happened against FC Copenhagen. Just like in the game against Lyngby, we were up 1-0 early but down 3-2 late. Ståle Solbakken scored two free-kicks in the last five minutes to turn it around again and give us a 4-3 victory. After the last goal, he ran to the sideline, grabbed one of the microphones that the TV companies used to record the sound from the field, and started singing and dancing with it. He was an awful dancer, but it was so funny that it became one of the most famous celebrations ever in Danish soccer.

We had a lot of games like that during the 1998-99 season. There was just an incredible belief in the team that, no matter what had happened, we could always bounce back. So when I conceded that goal against Lyngby, I still don't think any of us thought we would lose. We kept fighting, and with a few minutes left, Søren Frederiksen got the tying goal to make it 3-3.

At that point, news came through that we didn't even need to win our game because Brondby had lost again, 2-1 at home to Vejle. The title was ours. The last few minutes of our game were very awkward. We didn't really know what to do – we were just kicking the ball around waiting for the final whistle, and every time one of our players went near the referee, he would be tapping his wrists and shouting, "How much time, ref, how much time?" From where I was standing in goal, I could see the media were already lining up on the sideline. Backe was surrounded by photographers.

When the final whistle blew, the whole place went crazy. People were running everywhere and screaming. We stayed out on the pitch for a while to celebrate with the fans before we went back down to the locker room and found buckets of alcohol everywhere. I really don't drink often at all, but I had a couple of beers in the locker room, which was enough to get me drunk before we'd even left the stadium.

The team had organized a big, open-top bus to take us around the city immediately afterward, so it's a good thing the results went the right way! We came out of the locker room and just hopped right on. It felt like the whole city was following us as we drove around town with the trophy. I remember passing under traffic lights with fans hanging off them, reaching out to give us high-fives or shake our hands. The next day the newspapers reported there had been 55,000 people out in the streets, which would be about one-third of the city's total population.

We drove into town to this building that had a huge balcony, and we showed off the trophy. Then we got back on the bus and headed to a nightclub. I guess someone must have told the press, because when we pulled up there was an enormous crowd waiting outside. Those people were all over us as soon as we stepped off the bus – hugging us, kissing us, and literally tearing the clothes off our backs. They took my jacket, my shirt and my tie. By the time I got to the door of the club, I was standing there in my pants and nothing else.

I didn't care. I was so happy that day. It was an unbelievable feeling to win my first trophy, especially in my own town and at the stadium where I used to watch games when I was growing up. It's a completely different feeling than winning a big bet. This was something I had worked toward for years, putting in all those hours of practice, and it was something I had dreamt about as a little boy. I had some enormous wins at the casino over the years, which gave me a huge buzz for a few minutes afterward, but there was always a sense of "easy come, easy go." Winning the title wasn't easy. It was damn hard.

For me, nothing has ever compared to winning soccer games. I just don't get the same feeling from anything else. Becoming a father is a special moment, an unbelievable sensation and probably the best thing I have experienced in my life. But it is still a different feeling.

All of us players believed we would have many more triumphs to look forward to with Aalborg, but it wasn't to be. I was with the team for another eight years, but the closest I got to another trophy were those two cup finals that we lost in 2000 and 2004.

We had some good times, though, qualifying for European competition and playing against teams from across the continent. In fact, the year after we won the title, we just barely missed out on the Champions League, which is the highest level of European club soccer and worth a ton of money to the participating teams. The Danish

In Denmark, they don't let the league champions have the real trophy until after the season is finished. Because we secured first place with a week to spare, we had to use this modified replica when we went to celebrate with our fans. It was absolutely enormous – much bigger than the real thing – so it took a couple of us just to lift it. What a day that was, though, without doubt, one of the best of my career.

champions go through to a qualifying round for that tournament, and we drew Dynamo Kiev, the champions of Ukraine.

It was a two-legged qualifier, and we lost the first game at home, 2-1. Everybody thought we were out because Dynamo Kiev was a strong team at that time. They had just sold Andriy Shevchenko to Milan for about $25m, but they still had Serhiy Rebrov, who went on to play for Tottenham. They also had Oleh Luzhny, who later played for Arsenal, and a great goalkeeper named Oleksandr Shovkovsky.

But we went to Kiev for the return game and played our hearts out. With 15 minutes left, we were up 2-0, but then they got one back. It was 2-1 to us in the game, but it was 3-3 on aggregate across the two legs. In the 88th minute, we launched an attack. Jens Jessen got down to the goal line, swung a cross into the area, and Allan Gaarde scored. It was a goal that effectively counted double because we were not only up 4-3 on aggregate, but we had scored three of our goals away from home. In the Champions League, if the score is level after two legs, the team that has scored more goals away from home goes through.

We went crazy. Everybody on our bench came charging out onto the field, and I ran from my goal all the way down to the opposite corner where the guys were celebrating. Our players were all jumping on top of each other, and the few Danish fans who had traveled to Kiev were doing the same in the stands. But then we heard that whistle.

Peeeeeep! Peeeeeep! Peeeeeep! Peeeeeep! Peeeeeep!

I turned around and saw the linesman standing there with his flag up, saying that the ball had gone out of bounds before Jens delivered his assist to Allan. He was wrong, as it turned out. I watched the highlights later on that evening and the ball did not even touch the goal line, let alone cross it. But there was nothing we could do.

As if that wasn't bad enough, we conceded five minutes later. In the last minute of injury time, a cross came in from the left to find Maksim Shatskikh in the middle. He was only about two yards from goal, and I had no time to react to his shot, which finished up in the bottom corner. That made it 2-2 on the night, 4-3 to them on aggregate. Seconds later, the final whistle blew. After thinking we had won, we didn't even get to take the game to overtime.

That was one of the most disappointing days I had at Aalborg. We never got another chance to play in the Champions League because we never won the Danish title again. But we had some fun times in the UEFA Cup, which is the second-level European competition, before they rebranded it as the European League in 2009.

But at least I got to win that league title, which is not something everybody gets to do in their career. Now that I'm older, I have a much greater appreciation for what a big deal that was and how few players get the opportunity to do it, especially in their hometown. I gave the medal away to one of the team's fan clubs not long afterward, but I have all the memories I need, stored in my head.

12

HANS BACKE'S UNDERWEAR

I always had a lot of fun with my teammates at Aalborg, sometimes probably a bit too much. When we weren't out on the practice field or playing cards, then the other thing we seemed to spend our time doing was coming up with different practical jokes to play on each other.

A lot of it was little day-to-day pranks. We had a cream in Denmark called 303, which was the equivalent of Tiger Balm in the US. When you were tired after a practice session, you rubbed a little bit on your legs and it would make them go really hot, but it also stopped your muscles from aching.

We played around with that stuff a lot, putting it on people's clothes or rubbing it all over the bench in the sauna. That was the funniest because you wouldn't really notice it while you were in the sauna itself, and it would only be afterwards when you were driving home in your car that you'd suddenly realize, "Oh my God, my butt is burning." We stuck it in people's shoes sometimes, and then we would sit on the team bus betting on how long it would be before they took them off.

There were more elaborate pranks, too. In Denmark, there's a tradition of having a big hog roast around Christmas time, where you get the entire pig and cook it on a spit. The team organized a meal like that one year, and a few of us managed to sneak off with the pig's head afterward. Every player had a room at the team facility where we could sleep in the afternoon or sometimes the night before a game, so we took the pig's head and slipped it into a teammate's bed. When he went to lie down, he pulled back the covers and there it was, smiling up at him.

I was on the receiving end plenty of times. One time when we had a training camp in Cyprus, I was up playing cards with a few teammates in one of their rooms when they all started saying, "Oh, it's getting late, we should probably think about going to bed." I was surprised, because by our standards it was still quite early, but everybody else agreed that it was time to sleep, so I couldn't exactly carry on by myself.

I would usually have had a roommate for a trip like this, but we had an odd number of players in the squad that year and I was the lucky one who got my own room. I went back, brushed my teeth and got into bed. I still wasn't tired, so I had the TV on for a good 45 minutes before I finally switched it off, shut off the light and settled down to sleep.

I was just drifting away when suddenly I heard a noise. It woke me up with a start because it sounded like it had come from inside my room. Then I heard another one. I was freaking out at this point because the room was pitch-black and I couldn't see a thing. I spun around in my bed to reach for the light switch, but what I actually grabbed was a person's hand.

I get goose bumps thinking about it even now. I was terrified. All I remember is grabbing that hand as hard as I could and pulling it toward me, swinging punches into the darkness with my free arm and aiming where I guessed this person must be.

Finally, the person started shouting, "It's me! It's me! It's your teammate, Lars! We were trying to scare you!" I still couldn't stop right away. I don't know if it was because I was still panicked or if I was furious at him for doing that to me, but I hit him a few more times either way. He had been hiding in my closet the whole time, which was some pretty impressive dedication given how long he must have been in there between the end of the card game and me watching TV.

That card group was responsible for a lot of the pranks that went on. There were six or seven of us who played regularly, and for a long time we had a rule where the last hand of the day was not for money but instead to decide which one of us would do a forfeit.

More often than not it was something silly. A lot of times the rule would be that the loser had to run out of the team lineup as we came out on the field for Aalborg's next game and then sprint all the way down to the corner flag before coming back to join us at midfield. You had to do it really quickly because the manager came out right after the team, and you never wanted him to see.

The funniest one, though, came while Hans Backe was in charge. He would regularly have us do double practice sessions where we trained in the morning, took a break for lunch and trained again in the afternoon. So we had a few hours to kill in the middle of the day, before our second session, and more often than not we would spend it playing cards.

It was during one of those games – in between two practice sessions – that someone came up with a really crazy forfeit. The loser of the last hand should sneak into Hans Backe's office and try to steal the coach's underwear.

I don't know whose idea that was, but I do know my friend Jakob lost. The room we played cards in was on the third floor of the team's facility, down the corridor from Backe's office where we knew he and his assistant got changed every day before coming out to practice. We were pretty confident he wasn't in there; we hadn't heard anyone coming or going, but we couldn't be totally certain.

As Jakob left to undertake his mission, the rest of us crowded around the door of our room to watch. It was a long hallway with about twenty rooms coming off it, and Backe's office was right at the far end. We were all so nervous because the coach was such a hard-ass, and we had no idea what would happen if we got caught.

Finally, Jakob reached the far end of the corridor. He knocked on the door, making sure nobody was there, and after a few seconds he disappeared inside. He was probably only gone for a matter of seconds, but it felt like forever. Finally, the door burst open again and Jakob came sprinting out. He had the underwear – a pair of tighty whities – in his hand, and he was twirling them around his head with the end of his finger. We roared in celebration.

After that, stealing the coach's underwear became a regular forfeit for the next few days. Not only Backe's but his assistant's, too. We did it for three or four days running before they started locking the door of the office. We stopped for a little while, but then we persuaded the janitor to start opening it up for us again.

I had to steal them once myself. It was one of the most nerve-wracking things I have ever done. As you stood there outside his office, you would be trying to think up what you might say to him if he happened to be inside, what question you could ask to make it look like you were there for a legitimate reason.

Even if you had one of those legitimate reasons, Hans Backe's office was still a pretty scary place to be. There was one time during his spell in charge of Aalborg that I went to see him and really did have a question to ask about something we were doing in training. I knocked on the door and said, "Do you have thirty seconds?" He said yes, so I came in and started asking my question. Like everyone else, I was a bit scared of him, so I was talking a bit too much, going on and on like you do when you're around a person who makes you feel uncomfortable.

All of a sudden he interrupted me, saying, "Time's up," and then he just turned away from me. He never answered me or even looked at me again... he simply went back to his computer and ignored me. After standing there and feeling stupid for a few seconds, I had to slink back out. But that was what Hans Backe was like with everybody, and there was always a big distance between him and his players.

Thankfully, I only had to steal his underwear once. Usually that duty fell to Jakob because he wasn't very good at cards. None of us ever got caught, anyway, at least not by Backe. The only near miss was with the team's trainer. His room was on the same corridor, and one afternoon he was in there helping one of our teammates with some physio work. He must have heard us making noise outside and said, "What is going on out there?" The player who he was treating said, "Oh, they're going to steal Hans Backe's underwear again."

I don't know if the trainer really believed him at first, but he decided to go and look for himself. As usual, we were watching from the door of our room, and as he stepped out into the hallway we all had to dive back inside so he wouldn't see us. Then we were peeking round the door to see what he would do. He walked down the corridor to Backe's office and opened the door to find Jakob in there, looking for the underwear. We all rushed out at that point because we couldn't let Jakob take the fall on his own.

At first the trainer said he might have to tell Backe, but we were able to buy his silence with a nice dinner. After that episode, we stopped stealing the underwear and started coming up with some new forfeits. That near miss made us really think about how bad it might be if the coach ever found out. I guess he never did. Let's hope he never reads this book!

Photo courtesy AP Images

Hans Backe was a hard-ass but also a fantastic coach. He would have killed us if he found out about half the pranks we were up to, but we probably would have deserved it. We went too far sometimes.

13
GAMBLING GETS SERIOUS

My most successful night of gambling happened at a casino in Denmark. The place in question was a little drive away from Aalborg, and I had traveled there specifically that night so I could place some big bets away from prying eyes. Although I was still a regular at my old casino near home, if I wanted to bet really hard I always had to get out of town to make sure I wasn't going to run into anybody I knew or get spotted by the local reporters.

As usual, I went straight to the roulette table and started throwing down huge amounts of money right away. I had been winning a lot on my sports bets lately, so I had a plenty of cash in my pockets. I would have as much as $30,000 riding on a single spin of the wheel, which was the equivalent to almost two months' salary, though I didn't really think of it in those terms. When things were going well, I was careful to separate out my real money from my gambling money. It was only when things started to go badly that the line got blurred.

The luck was with me again that night. I kept winning and winning, the pile of chips in front of me getting bigger and bigger. People started to notice, and by the end of the night it felt like the whole casino was around my table watching me bet. It was a buzz, but I wasn't doing it to impress them. I was doing it because I wanted to win.

By the time I walked away from the table, I was up by more than $500,000. I had so many chips that I couldn't even carry them myself – every pocket of my suit was overflowing – and some of the staff had to help me take them over to the cashier. It was only a small casino, and they were totally unprepared for somebody to win that much money in a single evening. The cashier had to send for the manager, who arrived to tell me, "I'm so sorry, but we don't have that much money here. Can you come back to collect tomorrow?"

I have no reason to believe they were lying to me, but it would have been a very smart move if they were. I came back the next day to collect my winnings, and inevitably I decided to sit down at the roulette table again and bet a little more. I was probably only there for an hour and I lost about $350,000, more than half of what I had won the night before. When I finally walked out, I was still up by close to $150,000, but I felt like I had lost.

They wound up changing the law in Denmark not long after that night. Now all casinos are obliged to have the same amount of money in cash as they have out on the tables in chips. If there is $10m worth of chips in the casino, they need to have $10m in cash in their safe, specifically to avoid a situation like the one I had. I wouldn't assume it was because of what happened to me – I don't see how anybody would have known – but the law did change right afterward.

It was a funny moment being handed all that cash, even if I did give a lot of it straight back to the casino. They gave it to me in two plastic shopping bags with bundles and bundles of notes all thrown in with no great ceremony. I'm sure that would have freaked some people out, but I was accustomed to carrying around a lot of money at that time. I would easily have $20,000 in my pockets on an average day; I always wanted to be ready if I needed to place a bet. If I only had two or three grand on me, I felt broke.

And like I said, most of the time I kept my finances separate. I had my salary from soccer, which got paid into my main bank account, and then I had my gambling money. I never kept track of how far I was up or down with my betting, but I would know if I was doing well because I always stuffed my winnings into a little hiding place in the top of my closet, much like I did after that first big win at Millwall. If I'd had a good month, that space would be overflowing. If I'd had a bad month, there would be nothing there and I would have to find places to borrow money so I could keep going.

I could have two or three loans out from different banks and a couple more from my gambling buddies, too. Because I was a soccer player, everybody assumed I was good for it. And usually I was. As soon as I had a big win, I would go and pay them off. As a semi-professional gambler, you always had a few holes in your finances which you needed to plug whenever you got the chance.

My behavior over those two nights at the casino was also pretty typical, though. I was always winning big and then throwing my money away again. There was another time when I won $150,000 on a parlay (or an 'accumulator' as some people would call it), where you bet on a lot of different games all at once and you have to get every single one right. In effect, you turn lots of little bets into a single huge one.

The last result I needed was for the Spanish team, Valencia, to win its game by more than one goal. I watched it at the bookie. Valencia was up 1-0 in the 90th minute, and then it got awarded the luckiest penalty, which was scored. I asked the bookie to split my winnings onto two checks: one for $30,000, which was to repay some debts and another for $120,000. A few days later, I took the second check to the bank, cashed it and went straight to the casino. Within ten minutes, I had lost $20,000, and by the end of the night I had blown all the rest of it as well.

I was very good at hiding how much I had won or lost, to the point that not even my closest gambling buddies knew the extent of my betting. A lot of people tell me now that I'm very easy to read, that I wear my emotions on my sleeve. But I was always different with my betting. I had an incredible poker face, a "stone face" we would say in Denmark. I could be sitting opposite you and receive a text message telling me I had lost 100 grand, and you wouldn't know about it. I would glance down at my phone and take that news without a flinch.

Every now and then, though, something would slip out into the public domain. Like the time when I won 1.3 million Danish Krone ($240,000) betting on a parlay that included one of my own games.

Let me say straight away that I have *never* intentionally lost a game or conceded a goal in my life. There were lots of times when I could have done so, when it would have been the easiest thing in the world for me to throw a game and make the money I needed to pay off a debt here or there. But I never crossed that line; the thought didn't even enter my head. Both soccer and winning were too important to me, too sacred to even consider it.

This particular bet was part of a contest that the Danish bookies ran every week. They would publish a list of every game in Denmark's top two leagues, and for each one you had to pick home win, away win or tie. After that, it worked a bit like a lottery. If you got every game correct, you shared the money with everyone in the country who had done the same. If you picked 11 out of 12, you got a little less money.

There was also the option, though, to pay a bit more up front and pick multiple outcomes for the same game. So if there was one matchup you weren't sure about, you could hand over a little bit of extra cash when you entered the competition and select home win, away win and tie for that game. That way, you were always going to be correct on that particular game, regardless of the result.

So if I wanted to bet on that list, I would always pay the additional fee and make sure that I selected all three outcomes for Aalborg: home win, away win, and tie. That way, my performance for Aalborg didn't come into the equation at all; effectively I was just betting on the other eleven games.

It's a very hard bet to win. Even if you think you know a lot about soccer, there is almost always at least one team that gets a surprise result and kills your list. One week, though, I got lucky. I correctly called all eleven of the games not involving Aalborg, and for our game I was automatically correct because I had ticked every possible outcome. It turned out that I had been the only person in the entire country to make a clean sweep. The bad news was that we had lost our game that weekend.

A friend cashed the ticket in on my behalf, but somehow the story got out to the press. Suddenly, my phone was blowing up with calls from reporters asking, "Is this correct? Did you win all that money betting on your own game?" I tried to deny it, which probably wasn't the smartest move. The next day, there I was on the front page of the papers, under the headline: "Winning a million for losing." I couldn't believe it. I still had the slip showing that I had bet on all three results for our game, so I had to show that to everybody before they would believe that I hadn't done anything wrong. Even so, lots of people won't trust you after they've read a headline like that. I was fortunate that I had such a good relationship with our general manager, Lynge, because he stuck up for me as always, even if he did also tell me behind closed doors that I hadn't been very clever.

You would think that I might stop betting on that particular list afterward, but actually I had another big win, doing almost the exact same thing a year or two later. The only difference this time was that I had chosen a weekend when Aalborg wasn't playing, so there were only eleven games on the slip. The prize money was expected to be a bit smaller, but nobody could accuse me of doing anything wrong.

I remember that second win very well because Jannie and I had to go to a birthday party on the Sunday evening when the last of the games was being played. We were out at a nice restaurant, everyone sitting at this big long table, but I knew that I only needed one more result to win this bet, so I was constantly checking my phone and making up excuses to leave the table.

The bet was shared between me and one of my gambling buddies, so he was texting me updates. We needed a home win, but with 15 minutes left it was still 0-0. I didn't hear from him for what felt like a long time after that, so I began to assume that was the final score, but suddenly I got this message: "1-0! 1-0! 1-0!"

You didn't find out how much you had won straight away with that bet because they had to check to see how many people it was to be shared between. But an hour or two later I got a text from my friend saying, "Go where you can talk... right now!" I excused myself again to go to the bathroom and called him. He told me to sit down, so I had to go into one of the cubicles and perch on the end of a toilet. Finally he said, "We're the only winners! It's $260,000!"

I went crazy for a moment, cheering and celebrating, but then I had to straighten myself out and go back down to dinner without telling anyone. Looking back now, it's a fairly tragic scene – me in my smart clothes celebrating on my own while sitting on a toilet and then coming downstairs and hiding everything from the people who really cared about me. But back then it didn't feel tragic. I knew my family wouldn't approve, but I was winning and that was all that really mattered.

That's not to say I didn't care about their feelings, but I had convinced myself again that I wasn't really doing anything wrong. I had this mindset that what they didn't know wouldn't hurt them, which I realize now just wasn't true. Very often Jannie would know that I was lying to her, but she didn't know what she could do about it.

And the longer it went on, the more selfish I got. Ever since that first trip to Las Vegas with Jannie, I had been obsessed with going back, so a few years later, when Aalborg had a bye week, I suggested to one of my gambling buddies that we should go spend a few days out there. I had Thursday to Sunday off because of the bye, so when my practice finished on Wednesday we went straight to the airport and got on a plane. We hadn't planned it in advance at all. We simply decided then and there that we should do it.

My phone didn't work in America, and I didn't tell anybody I was leaving, not even Jannie. We flew out to Vegas and I gambled like crazy for four days solid. I was betting so much that the casino – Treasure Island, again – started giving us all sorts of free stuff, upgrading our room to a huge suite and handing us free tickets to see Cirque du Soleil. We gave those tickets away to two strangers and kept on gambling. I don't think I set foot outside the casino the whole time I was there. Treasure Island has a big pirate ship out front where they do shows outside every few hours, with cannons going off and explosions, but I wasn't interested. The most I saw of that was on the cab ride back to the airport.

I lost a ton of money on that trip, and on the plane back, I remember feeling like the worst person ever. By the time I landed, I had all these messages on my phone, not only from Jannie but also my mom and dad. Everybody was getting scared about what had happened to me because it was as if I had disappeared off the face of the earth. In the end, Jannie had heard about our trip through someone my friend told; he had at least thought to let people know where we were going.

It's hard for me to explain now what was going through my head when I did things like that. When I got that urge to gamble, it was like nothing else mattered any more, I had to go and satisfy that right away or else it would drive me crazy. I always felt like I was under pressure to make that next bet. I had this fear that if I didn't make it, then I might miss a chance to win. With all that going on in my brain, it was like there was no room for anything or anybody else. I was addicted, even though I wouldn't have acknowledged it at the time.

I had one more trip to Vegas after that, this time for just 18 hours. I didn't even bring a suitcase. I got off the plane, went to the casino and gambled until it was time for my flight home. That was insane, since it took more than 18 hours to fly one-way from Aalborg to Vegas. The whole round-trip took almost three days, but less than a third of that was actually spent at the destination.

But casinos in Denmark were too small, too quiet, and sometimes I needed the action to be a little bit faster. The other thing I would do when I felt like that was to head across the border into Germany. There was a nice casino in Hamburg, about a five-hour drive away.

The rest of the time I would be on the phone with my bookie. I was still using the same betting shop that I first went to when my dad's place shut down, but I didn't always have to go there in person any

Where else could this be but Las Vegas? This photo was taken during the first trip I ever made to the city with Jannie, though neither of us really cared that much about the slot machines. I always wanted to be at the roulette tables where the stakes were higher, and Jannie just wasn't that interested in gambling at all.

131

more. I had built up a strong relationship over time with the owner, Jørgen, so I could just phone him whenever I wanted to put a bet on. He knew I always paid my debts, so he let me do it all on credit. I'd say, "I want $10,000 on this match," he'd go, "OK," and then whatever happened, we would settle things up financially a few days later.

Jørgen was a good guy, very calm and extremely loyal. He had known me since I was a kid because my dad used to gamble with him, but he never told anyone in my family about what I was betting. That was between me and him.

I had a lot of good luck with my betting in those first two years after I got married. I was winning big sums of money – $100,000 or more – on a regular basis, but the problem is that once you've started doing that, you don't ever want to take a step back. To win $100,000 you usually have to place bets of at least $10,000, and I could do that several times in a single day. Every morning I would wake up and do my research, but if my first big bet of the day didn't come off, I would keep placing more and more to try to make up for it.

It wasn't enough to have a Plan A; there needed to be a Plan B, a Plan C, a Plan D. Put it this way: I had to know the whole alphabet. And when I was getting desperate for that win, I would start betting on sports that I knew absolutely nothing about, like volleyball, swimming, or rugby games in countries that I can't even pronounce.

I've asked myself lots of times how much money I must have lost in total, but it makes me feel sick even thinking about it. It must be millions of dollars if you count everything I won and then threw away again. The stupid part is that the money didn't even really mean anything to me at that point. I wasn't using it to finance a lavish lifestyle or anything like that. I never rushed out after a big win and bought a Ferrari, and I didn't hang out in clubs buying $5,000 bottles of champagne. The money was merely a way of keeping score, like in a game of Monopoly. I took it and hid it away in my closet until I needed to play with it again.

For a few years, everything worked out fine. Like any other gambler, I had ups and downs, but despite behaving recklessly at times, I continued to win more than I lost. My soccer money stayed separate from my gambling money, and the former went toward my life with Jannie and Mille. We bought a nice three-bedroom house together and lived comfortably, nothing crazy – a soccer player's salary in Denmark still wasn't like it would be in England or Spain – but we did OK.

As I mentioned, I even had enough money to do something that I had always dreamed of: owning shares in a few racehorses. That turned out to be a very expensive hobby. It's not so much about what you pay for the horse up front as it is the bills you have to pay for the stables, the trainer, the vet and the food. It was nearly as expensive as transporting a gerbil to America!

I had seven or eight different horses over the years, all of them co-owned with different people. There were a couple that I shared with my family and Jannie's family, others with friends, and some that I had with my bookie. It was a lot of fun to go to the track and watch your own horse race – not that mine ever won. We had some terrible horses. The only one that was any good got homesick as soon as you took him away from his stable, so we couldn't get him to run anywhere except the local track. The trainer told us it was because he missed the horse in the stable next to him, so we tried transporting that horse along to all of his races, but that didn't help, either, and it just cost us even more money.

In the end, I think we wound up giving away every one of the horses I owned to families who wanted one as a pet, because not one of them was any good at racing. I lost a bit of money betting on them at the track, but much more paying for all of their bills. Even so, I have to admit that I would love to own another horse again one day. I do love watching them race.

There are more stories I could tell about my gambling life in those years, but they would only be variations on a theme. I risked too much, took my loved ones for granted and made too many bad decisions to ever recount. And before 2004, I had absolutely no plans to stop. That was the year when things finally began to spiral out of my control.

14
ROCK BOTTOM

Outside of the card games, there was only one teammate at Aalborg who I gambled with regularly. David Nielsen joined Aalborg from Norwich City, of all teams, in 2003, and we hit it off right away. Despite our shared surname, we weren't related, but we certainly had a lot in common. He was a forward with a very different job from mine, but we shared that competitiveness and need to win at everything we did. David also liked to gamble on sport, so it wasn't long before he came to me asking for advice about a good bookie.

I told him about Jørgen and put the two of them in touch. I also spoke to Jørgen separately, telling him, "David is a good guy. When he calls up to place a bet, you can trust him, he's good for it." In hindsight, that was probably a silly thing for me to say about a guy who I had only just met. But for a long time, I was right – Jørgen could trust him. There was even one time when David bailed me out, loaning me $20,000 to repay the bookie at a point when I was struggling to get the money together.

David was a very colorful person who had a lot of positive energy around him. He was so funny and full of life that you wanted to be around him the whole time. When you were in his company, it felt like you were flying along with him. We got on very well, and for the first year after David joined the team, it became our regular thing to head down to the bookie together after practice. If there was a game on in the evening, we might stay there all afternoon, placing our bets and exchanging notes on the research we had done.

At a certain point, though, things started to turn against us. I cannot point to a single moment – it doesn't work like that when you're gambling every day – but something changed and it felt like I couldn't pick a winner anymore. Day after day, week after week, I was losing more money than I was winning. I responded by raising the stakes even higher, telling myself that if I could land one big bet, it would fix all my problems at a stroke. Instead, that only made things worse, increasing the speed at which I was driving myself bankrupt.

I had always kept my promises to Jørgen. Any time I'd asked him for an extra few days to pay a debt, he had always said yes, and I had always got the money to him when I told him I would. But this time, I couldn't seem to turn things around. By April 2004, I owed him $60,000, which might not sound like a lot – given the scale of my gambling – but I had exhausted all of my other funds simply to keep the debt down to that level.

My various loans from banks and private lenders added up to more than a quarter of a million dollars. Most of them were pushing me for overdue repayments, too. In desperation, I had also broken down that wall between my soccer income and my gambling money, clearing out my entire personal bank account and the joint savings I had with Jannie. It wouldn't have mattered if I owed Jørgen $100 or $100,000,000, I was broke, and there was simply no way for me to raise any more money.

What made the situation even worse was that David was having a similar problem at the exact same moment. He owed Jørgen more than I did – I don't know exactly how much – and our combined debt made the situation impossible for Jørgen.

All bookies in Denmark operate under license from the government, so when you place a bet in your local shop, they are effectively serving as the middle man between you and a big central betting company, which is called Tipstjeneste. When you win, the bookie pays you and then claims the money back from that central body. But when you lose, they have to pay Tipstjeneste on your behalf, keeping a small percentage for themselves.

Jørgen had been placing these bets on our behalf, relying on the belief that we could pay him back as we always did. But now that we had left him out of pocket, he was unable to cover his own debts to Tipstjeneste. We had already persuaded him to give us a little extra time, telling him we would both pay him on a particular day, but when that day rolled around, neither of us had the money. I remember sitting in my car with David outside practice, looking at each other and not knowing what to do. We were in deep, deep trouble.

I had one last idea about how I could raise the money. When we won the league in 1999, Aalborg gave all of the players a bonus and I had used mine to buy some shares in the club. There were rules that prevented employees from selling those whenever we wanted to, but I knew that if Jørgen could hold on for three more weeks, there was a date coming up when I would be able to off-load them. They weren't worth enough to clear all my financial problems – not even close – but combined with my next wage packet, it would be enough to settle my debt to Jørgen.

David and I drove down to the betting shop together. Because I had known Jørgen longer, I took the lead. I told him, "I know it's supposed to be payday, but we can't get this money to you right now. If you can hang on three more weeks, I promise to have everything I owe you."

He couldn't wait that long. "I need the money tomorrow," he said, and we went back and forth for the next few minutes. He was in no position to be flexible – he needed to pay off his own debts – but there was simply no way for either me or David to raise the funds in time. I left, still promising him his money. Two days later, the store shut down.

There was no big announcement, Jørgen simply stopped opening up his doors. With Aalborg being the size it is, word quickly got around. Right away, people were asking me if I knew what was going on. They all were aware that I had a good relationship with the owner, but I told them I had no idea. I felt bad, but I kept telling myself that it wasn't the end of the world. I believed I was going to find a way to pay Jørgen and make it right.

The longer the shop stayed shut, though, the worse I began to feel. Lynge had asked me point-blank on the day the news came out whether I had anything to do with it. I told him, "No, it's nothing to do with me." But a day later, as I drove away from practice, I realized I had to come clean. I swung the car around and went straight to his office. I said, "This needs to be between you and me," then I told him everything. I knew after my wedding that I could trust him to keep a secret.

As I've said before, he was not someone who rushed his judgments. He thanked me for being honest and told me that he would think about what we could do next to try to fix this problem. A bit like my dad on the night of the Casino Jimmy incident with the U-21 team, Lynge didn't tell me off, because I think he could see that I was already sorry enough about what had happened.

That night, though, Lynge called me with some bad news. "A newspaper has got the story," he said. "They know it was you and David who shut down the bookie, and they're going to run a big piece about it in tomorrow's edition. You better tell the people who need to know about this before they read about it in the morning."

It was already 7:00 p.m., and I started telling him, "I can't do that, I'm not going to be able to get hold of everybody," but there was nothing he could do. That story was coming whether we wanted it or not, and it was up to me to decide how my family and friends got to hear about it first.

The first thing I did after hanging up that call was curse – *a lot*. But after a few seconds getting it out of my system, I knew where I had to start. I went to find Jannie, who already knew something was up. She had asked me about the bookie the day before, but I had lied to her just like I did to everybody else. Now I started to tell her, "You know I've been gambling quite a lot lately?"

"Yes…"

"You know that I've had some pretty bad luck?"

"Yes…"

"And you know that the bookie shut down?"

She must have known where I was going from the second I opened my mouth, but I couldn't get the words out quickly. Even as I was speaking, I was still trying to work out how I could break this news to her, how to explain that I had blown everything we had worked so hard to build up together. Now she cut in, saying, "I asked you a few days ago if you knew what was going on there and you told me you didn't."

"Yes, I know. I was lying. I owe the bookie some money together with another guy off the team, and right now I can't pay him."

She took that part in stride.

"OK, take the money from our savings."

"I can't. I already spent it all."

She started crying at that point, but she still didn't know half the story. I had only told her about the bookie and the empty savings account, not the hundreds of thousands of dollars' worth of debt I had with all of the other banks.

I was sure Jannie would walk out on me that night. I couldn't have blamed her if she did, given all the things you already know about how

I had treated her. She had left once before, a couple of years earlier, after finding out that I had once again been hiding the extent of my gambling. I had been going through another rough patch and started getting warning letters from some of the banks about overdue payments.

Jannie was working as a secretary at that time, so I knew that if I rushed home right after practice, I could pick up the mail before her. If I had double sessions, I would drive home in the middle of the day to check for any letters, and if there were some that I didn't want her to see, I would hide them away in the drawer of my desk.

But for whatever reason, I failed to make it home one day, and she found a letter that revealed some debt I hadn't told her about. As usual, it was only the tip of the iceberg, but between that and the way I had been treating her – disappearing off gambling without warning or explanation – she decided to take some time out, going to stay with her parents for a while and taking Mille with her. She came back a few weeks later, after I had apologized and promised to change, which was yet another promise I failed to keep. It helped that my betting fortunes had improved in the meantime, so I could show her that debt had been cleared.

This time she didn't leave. In fact, even though she was upset, she stuck up for me and defended me that night and in the weeks that followed. Later on, and only when there was nobody else around, she would pull no punches, telling me exactly how much I had let her and Mille down and how it made her feel. But nobody else was allowed to talk to me that way. If she heard anybody else criticizing me, she would go after them with a fury. I will never be able to thank her enough for the way she stuck by me and fought in my corner. I had done nothing to deserve that kind of loyalty.

It didn't make that night any less awful, though. If ever I needed a reality check about my gambling and the impact it had on other people, this was it. Imagine making a list of all the people who care about you and calling them one by one just so you could tell them something that was going to make them sad, angry and upset. That was exactly what I had to do, saying the same thing every time: "Most of what you read about me in tomorrow morning's newspapers is going to be true."

The worst was my mom. I told her to come over rather than trying to explain on the phone. When she got there, I sat down with her on the couch and explained. She got very upset, cried a lot, but also got very angry, which I didn't expect. Normally when I did wrong, she would be more disappointed, but this time she was mad at me as well.

She had every right to be. Both my mom and Jannie had at different times persuaded me to see a therapist about my gambling. I agreed for the sake of keeping them happy, and I told them at the time that it was really helping, but in reality, I had never taken it seriously at all. I even went to the casino on the way back from the therapist's office a few times.

My dad came round, too, as did some of Jannie's family. When I was done with all my phone calls, we just sat there in the front room, and I don't think anybody really knew what to say anymore. I didn't want anyone's help with the money because I knew I could sell those shares in the club and pay off my debt to the bookie. I hadn't told anybody about the rest of the money I owed. I'd love to tell you that this moment was the great epiphany where I realized I had to come clean and change my ways, but that isn't true. As terrible as I felt that night, and as much as I hated myself for letting all those people down, I still believed 100% that I was just one good bet from turning things around.

The next day, Aalborg hosted a press conference at the practice facility. David and I faced the media together, but even though his debts to the bookie were much bigger, the reporters were more interested in my role. After the Casino Jimmy incident and that story with me betting on my own game, this was like throwing petrol on a fire.

I remember sitting there and saying over and over again that I was going to pay Jørgen everything I owed him. And three weeks later, I did. He opened the betting shop up again for a few days, but David still wasn't able to repay him, and before long, it shut down again. On that front, at least, I felt able to walk away with a clear conscience.

It's very hard to enforce gambling debt under Danish law, so there would have been no real repercussions for me if I hadn't repaid Jørgen. But I gave him his money like I told him I would, even if it was a little late. It was always extremely important to me that I paid off my debts. I got cheated a few times in my life by people I bet with, and it was a horrible experience. I never wanted to be the person doing that to someone else.

I couldn't clear my other debts quite so easily, though. The bills kept piling up at home, and it was getting harder and harder to hide everything from Jannie. Once again, I was driving back home between practice sessions, racing back to pick up that mail and protect this double life I had been leading. Even after everything that had come out in the press over those few days, I still felt like I had to preserve it, to find a way of turning things around and getting back to how we were before.

But the debts were too big now, impossible to hide, and my usual method for fixing it – placing more bets – couldn't work anymore, because after the story went public, there was nobody in the whole city stupid enough to lend me money. More than anything else, that was what really stopped me from going back to gambling, the simple fact that I couldn't get my hands on any money to do it with.

Aalborg's main sponsor at that time was a bank called Spar Nord, and as luck would have it, they were about the only bank in the city that I didn't already have loans out with. Lynge spoke to someone there about my situation, and they offered to have one of their managers take a complete overview of my finances and see what could be done. I was so relieved. It was a dream solution: Spar Nord could buy out all of my existing loans and simplify everything into one monthly repayment out of my salary.

My teammate and former bookie partner, David Nielsen. He left Aalborg in 2005, but I saw him again a few years later when we took a coaching course together. David, like me, made some poor decisions with his betting, but I still say he was a good guy and a fantastic soccer player.

141

Or at least that was how I imagined it was going to go. Over the next few days, I gave Spar Nord all the information they asked for, coming completely clean about all the different debts I had. Not long after that, I got a phone call from one of the bank's directors, telling me they had looked through everything and asking if I could come in for a meeting that evening. Jannie and I went there together, and when we arrived, there was food out and everybody was smiling and saying hello. I thought, *This is going to be brilliant. This is the moment where I get to start over and turn my life around.*

It wasn't. As soon as we sat down, the director's tone changed. "OK, let's get to the serious part," he said. "Having looked through your finances, I can safely say that we would not touch you as a client. This is the biggest mess I have seen in my entire life."

He placed his fingers on the corner of the table, tilting them backwards like a man looking over the edge of a cliff. "This is how precarious your situation is," he continued. "You are on the brink of going completely bankrupt. You are tiptoeing right along the edge, and if you make one wrong step, you are going to fall so far that nobody will ever lend you anything ever again. If you spend so much as five krone wrong, you will be finished."

He went on to give us some advice about what we should do next, which involved selling our house and pretty much everything else we owned, as well as cutting back our spending in every area you could imagine. But that was as much help as Spar Nord was prepared to give us.

We walked out of there shell-shocked. For the first time in a long, long time, I didn't have a backup plan; I didn't have a Plan B, much less a Plan C or a Plan D. I had put all my hopes on that bank helping us to find a solution, and that was all I had. We got as far as the car before Jannie broke down. She had cried a little the night I told her about the bookie, but now she was sobbing uncontrollably.

I started crying, too. I'm not someone who cries often, and I could probably count on the fingers of one hand the number of times I can remember doing so. I don't say that to show off, and I don't think that makes me more of a man or anything like that. It's just the truth. But now the tears were flowing. I was lost. I had no idea how to get out of this mess I had created. Or if I ever would.

15
REHAB

We sold our house as the bank had advised. It was a nice, three-bedroom place in a good area, but I had so many loans out that it barely made a dent in what we owed. My mom and dad were no longer living together by then, but my father offered to let us have his place while we got back on our feet. He rented another, smaller apartment in Aalborg while we were there.

I wanted to say no, because it was unfair to him and humiliating for me to admit I needed his charity. But the truth was that we had no choice. I have no idea how we would even have survived without the help we got from our families over the next few months. We had to sell everything: our house, the furniture, my car... everything. I had to borrow a bike and cycle in to practice every morning, about a thirty-minute ride. Our parents came round every few days to take us out grocery shopping. In Denmark, you can earn ten cents for recycling glass soda bottles, so I collected those in my time off after practice. That's not a thing to be ashamed of, but for someone who was used to walking round with thousands of dollars in his pockets, it was certainly a long way to fall.

Aalborg was unbelievable with me. Lynge gave me a new contract with improved wages and a new signing-on fee. That wasn't just charity from Aalborg, because despite everything, I was still playing well. I have this technique which I use during games, where I think of myself like a movie director. If something bad happens, I cut that scene out and keep the better ones in my mind. Now I was doing the same thing with regard to my life off the field. While I was playing, I could cut out the thoughts I didn't need and focus on doing my job.

143

Still, it was good of the team to give me a new contract in the middle of a season. They didn't have to do that. The signing bonus allowed me to reduce the overall debt slightly, and the wage increase meant I could at least meet the minimum payments on my loans. Much like when I was working at my dad's bookie as a teenager, I never saw my paycheck; every month it just disappeared toward paying off those debts I had built up.

The urge to gamble didn't disappear overnight. I still had this idea in my head that I only needed to make one more bet, that I could put everything right with a single long-odds winner. I would daydream about winning so much money that we could buy a new house and avoid all these needless years of suffering. *One bet, one win, and it's all gone.*

There was no way for me to act on that impulse, though, because I had no money to bet with. I was totally broke, and, as I said, after that story made the papers, nobody in Aalborg would lend me anything. I couldn't go into a bank and make up a story about needing another new kitchen, because they all knew exactly what was going on.

It was probably the best thing that could have happened to me. The one time I did manage to get my hands on some money, I blew it yet again.

A few months after the bookie shut down, I was supposed to go on a golfing holiday with some teammates in Spain. The whole thing was paid for in advance, so after discussing it with my wife, we agreed that I might as well still go. Jannie's parents owned a holiday home near the golf resort, so the plan was for me to play golf for a few days with my buddies before they went home and before she flew out to join me for our wedding anniversary. After everything that had happened, it felt like the break could do us some good.

Thanks to an agreement we signed before getting married, Jannie had always kept a part of her finances separate from mine. She was working as a secretary at that time and only had a modest salary, but it was her money that we lived on while my wages were being used to pay off the debts. When I flew out to Spain, she gave me her bank card to cover any emergency expenses.

Instead, I used it to go to a casino. For three days running, I woke up, played golf with my buddies, had some dinner and then headed out to gamble with Jannie's money. As usual, I was not doing a good job of keeping track, but I knew I was losing more money than I was winning.

When Jannie arrived, we went out for dinner and had a wonderful evening. But on the way back to her parents' holiday home, I got pulled over for speeding. The policeman ordered me to pay a €70 ($95) fine. I didn't have enough on me, so he told me to drive to the nearest ATM, following us there on his motorbike. I put my wife's card into the machine, only for a message to flash up that too much money had already been drawn from the account. I stood there not knowing what to do. I wasn't afraid of the cop, but I was afraid of having to explain the situation to my wife.

She must have worked it out for herself because after a few minutes, she got out of the car, walked over and pushed me aside. Jannie had one more card she could use and managed to take enough out to pay the policeman. I had a lot of explaining to do on the drive back. That was another anniversary I ruined.

Not long afterward, Jannie and her mother staged a little intervention. I was leaving practice one day when I got a phone call from Lynge. He said he was in his office with both of them and that I needed to come back in so we could all talk. I was angry at first – I felt like I was being ambushed – but after a second, I spun the car around and drove back to the facility.

I had been going to rehab ever since the night when I came clean about the bookie, but the incident in Spain made it clear things still weren't working. Lynge gave it to me straight: If I didn't change immediately, I was going to lose something much more important than money. I was going to drive away the people who loved me, once and for all.

He agreed to help me find a new therapist. I had never felt any connection to any of the people I had spoken to so far; they always seemed more interested in keeping one eye on the clock than listening to what I had to say. They didn't care about me, so I didn't tell them the truth. I would sit there for an hour and say whatever I thought they wanted to hear.

Lynge put me in touch with another guy, Bjorn, but I knew I was going to have to do things differently for this to work. I told Bjorn up front that I wasn't happy coming into his office, which was right in the middle of town. I didn't like the fact that people could see you going in there and know what you were doing. Instead, I asked if we could meet at his home, and he said that would be fine.

Bjorn lived out in the countryside at least an hour outside of Aalborg, and the first time I drove out there, he had to come meet me on the main road to guide me through the last bit of the journey. The place he directed me to was not his house, but a disused circus wagon sitting in a field he owned. It was an unbelievable place, the outside still painted up in the colors of the circus, but the inside laid out like somebody's front room, with a fireplace and some chairs. As we got further into winter, he would load more and more logs onto the fire.

I loved having our sessions in there. It didn't feel like you were in rehab at all, but instead like you had taken yourself away to a different part of the planet. I felt comfortable, and maybe that helped me to speak honestly. But the most important thing was Bjorn himself. From the very first time we spoke, I felt a connection unlike anything I had enjoyed with my previous therapists. He talked to me like I was a person, rather than a customer.

He also listened – *really* listened – to what I had to say. It's hard to explain quite what a relief it was to finally have someone who I could tell everything without worrying that I was going to make them sad. Every time I walked out of that wagon, I felt physically lighter, as though a weight had literally been lifted off my shoulders.

Even though Jannie knew about my debts by now, there were still so many things I hadn't told her yet, so many lies to unpick from years spent trying to cover up my gambilng. Over time, Bjorn taught me how to explain things to her, helping me choose the right words to use when addressing my family, my friends and even the media. But to start with, I was happy just to have found one person I could speak honestly to. Whenever I got home from one of those sessions, Jannie would want to know what we had spoken about, but I had to ask her to wait and be patient – as if she hadn't already done that enough! Gradually I did tell her everything, but it would have been too much for both of us to do it all in one go.

My meetings with Bjorn carried on for nine or ten months. At first I saw him several times a week, but toward the end we reduced that to once a week, then once a fortnight. The toughest part was working out what to do with all my spare time. As I've said before, you get a lot of that as a soccer player, and the most difficult part of the day for me was always right after practice. In the past, I would have come home and spent that time studying the form guides and deciding what bets to place.

Now I slept. For the first few months after the bookie shut down, I would get home in the afternoon and go straight to bed, partly because I didn't know what else to do but also because ever since the gambling stopped, I found myself feeling totally exhausted. I spoke about that with Bjorn, too, saying, "Listen, I'm a young man, but I'm living like a guy in his late 70s. I come home from practice and sleep for three or four hours." He told me that was normal for someone in withdrawal and reassured me that I would get to the other side. But as long as I felt like sleeping, he told me to sleep.

As my energy levels returned, Bjorn gave me some suggestions of other ways to fill the time, such as taking the dog for a walk. I swear to God, the dog we had back then must have been the fittest pet on the planet. Most dogs are excited when you tell them it's time for a walk, but that dog was so exhausted, I usually had to drag it out the door.

I often get asked if I have any advice for other people who find themselves in a similar situation. The answer is that I definitely do, but it's nothing as straightforward as saying, "Walk your dog every day and that will keep you from placing a bet." Everything is individual, and there's no one thing I can say that would work for everybody. I would have to talk to the person and understand their situation before I would feel comfortable telling them to try something that I did.

But walking the dog worked for me. As I walked, my thoughts gradually turned to different things, whether it was thinking up fun activities to do with the kids or worrying about some other problem besides gambling. Most importantly, though, it gave me somewhere to be other than sitting at my desk and researching bets, or down at the bookie putting them on.

I don't want to make it sound like any of this came easily, though. Every single day was a battle, pushing myself to do something – anything – other than placing a bet. You have to change every single one of your routines, as well as your social circle. I had friends who had done nothing wrong, who liked to gamble casually – not to the excess like I did – and who I couldn't spend time with any more. I had to stay away from that whole environment.

I used to have a subscription to a magazine named *Tipsbladet*, which is the biggest sports publication in Denmark. It isn't all about gambling, but it has a small section about it in each edition, and I knew exactly what pages it would be on. It comes out twice a week, Tuesday and Friday, and before the incident with the bookie, I would collect my copy from our mailbox on my way to practice.

Now I couldn't even look at it. If I was out somewhere and saw a copy lying on a table, I would find myself leaning over, trying to lift up one corner and sneak a peek at the gambling page. Sometimes I would catch a glimpse of a particular bet with great odds and that old thought would come straight back into my head: *If I put enough money on, at those odds, I could wipe out all of my debt in one go.*

After that trip to Spain, though, I always managed to resist. Bjorn would say, "If you ever find yourself thinking seriously about placing another bet, then do yourself and me a big favor: call me before you do it." And there were a few times when I did exactly that. He was very good at reminding me of the things I had told him about why I wanted to stop.

Bjorn wasn't the only person I could call, though. There was one night when I was feeling especially low and couldn't see any light at the end of the tunnel. Instead of Bjorn, I phoned Lynge. It was 11:30 and he was already asleep, but I said, "I need to talk to you and it can't wait until tomorrow," and he replied, "OK, I'll get out of bed, put the coffee on and see you when you're ready."

I drove straight over there. We spent the whole night talking not only about gambling, but about life in general. I no longer knew where my life was headed. I had spent my whole childhood dreaming of being a soccer player, but now that I had achieved that part, I wasn't sure if it was enough. In the early part of my career, there had been all that talk of a move to Manchester United or some other big team in Europe, but it never happened. Now I was playing for the club I supported all my life, had won a league title, yet I didn't know if I should be satisfied or disappointed.

Lynge stayed up with me right through to morning, sitting and listening. I'm sure he gave me some great advice, too, just like he always did. But what stays with me more than anything is the simple fact that he was willing to give up a night's sleep to listen to me talk. How many bosses would do that for one of their employees?

I was incredibly lucky to have people like that around me. Were it not for the support network that I had – my wife, my daughter, Bjorn and Lynge – I wonder if I really would have stopped at all, or if I would have kept on gambling until they threw me out on the street or somebody killed me for failing to pay off a debt. It's a horrible thought, but is it that unrealistic? I know how long I had that thought in my head, that constant nagging desire to place one more bet.

To be 100% truthful, that thought never goes completely away. When we finally paid off the last of my debts a few years later, I immediately started to feel a lot more relaxed about it because I could stop putting

Lynge Jakobsen: general manager of Aalborg, and my second dad. He has done so much for me throughout my career, but especially after everything came to a head with my gambling. He was the one who set me up with my therapist, Bjorn, and Lynge also gave up countless hours of his own time helping me to talk through my problems. I will never be able to thank him enough.

myself under pressure to fix the mess I had made. Even now, though, there are times when a game will come on TV and I'll hear the little voice in the back of my head saying, *it'd be fun to have a bet on this.* It's just that I have techniques now for getting past that, ways to distract myself until the thought goes away.

Quitting gambling was not just about fighting my own demons. It took years to build up the trust in my relationship with Jannie again. Back when I was gambling, I used to keep my betting slips in the back pocket of my pants, and for a long time afterward she would sneak up on me and stick her hand in there to see if I was carrying any. Her touch went through me like lightning, because for years I always felt like I did have something in there, even though I didn't. I'd think: *Oh my God, she caught me,* before I could remind myself that I hadn't done anything wrong.

With time, though, things began to improve. Each month we paid off a little more of that debt, and each night I went to bed having survived another day without a bet. Finally I could see a speck of light at the end of that tunnel, even if it was still a long way off.

16
THE WRONG MOVE

A few weeks after the bookie shut down, I lost my third Danish Cup final with Aalborg, against FC Copenhagen. Three days later, we had to play the same team again in the league. There were only two games left in the season, and we were fifth, with no chance of winning the league or getting relegated. Copenhagen, on the other hand, was involved in a very tight race for the title, along with Brondby.

The winners of the Danish Cup normally went into the UEFA Cup, but if Copenhagen won the league, that would earn them entry into the Champions League qualifying rounds instead, and we would take their UEFA Cup spot. That put us in a difficult position. If we beat them in that league game, we were effectively damaging our own chances of playing in European competition the following season.

It was an extremely strange feeling stepping out onto the field that day. Copenhagen's stadium was packed with nearly 40,000 people, and normally, I love to play in games like that. This time, though, I didn't even want to run onto the field because the whole situation was just too confusing. Once the game started, however, we set about trying to win it because that was the right thing to do.

After a few minutes we went up 1-0, but then David Nielsen missed one of the biggest chances I have ever seen. Copenhagen scored a tying goal late in the game and it finished 1-1. That was enough to keep Copenhagen on top by one point with one game left to go.

As we were walking off the pitch, David told me he'd missed his shot on purpose. I was furious with him for saying that. I told him to shut up and that I wished he hadn't told me. As much as I could understand his logic, I have never tried to not win a game of soccer.

The final outcome might have been good for us, but I wanted to believe we had got there the right way.

I buried my head in the sand at that point, not saying anything to anyone, because frankly, David and I had enough bad publicity already. A few years later, he wrote about it in his own autobiography, and that caused a bit of a storm. But I want to be absolutely clear that I had nothing to do with it. David was his own man, and as far as I am aware, everybody else on that team was trying to win the game, exactly like I was.

In the end, Copenhagen did win the league and we got the UEFA Cup spot. About a year later, David got kicked off the team after getting into a bad fight with another of our teammates in practice. That was a shame because he was a nice guy, but he did make some poor decisions.

Otherwise, from a soccer perspective, those years were largely uneventful. We finished fifth in the league in 2004 and it was a similar story for the next few years: fourth in 2005, fifth in 2006, then third in 2007. We were always in that top part of the table but never really challenging for the title.

I still wasn't sure how to feel about my career. I was caught between pride at what I had achieved yet always wondering how different things would have been if I had landed that big transfer. But I never got bored with playing soccer itself. I still loved the sport and never missed a game.

There is one particular story which might give you some idea of how important soccer was to me. It was early 2006, and we had a game coming up in a tournament called the Royal League, which includes teams from across Denmark, Sweden and Norway. Jannie was a few months pregnant with our second child. There had been a few complications, but the doctors said the most important thing was that she relax and not try to do too much. So I left Jannie with her parents and got ready to go to our Royal League game against Lyn Oslo, a team from Norway.

We had a short flight from Aalborg to Copenhagen before changing onto another plane for the trip to Oslo. It was only a short layover, so I was already standing at the boarding gate in Copenhagen when I checked my phone. As soon as I turned it on, it started buzzing away, showing a ridiculous number of missed calls from my mother-in-law.

I stepped out of the line to phone her back and immediately heard in her voice that something was wrong. "I'm afraid Jannie might have lost the baby," she said. "She's at the hospital right now, and I think you better come back."

As you may remember from my incident at the casino with the Danish U-21 team, it's a four-hour drive from Copenhagen to Aalborg. I told Lynge what had happened and we both ran straight over to the desk of the airline we were flying with – SAS – to see if there were any flights going back in that direction. At first the lady behind the desk said no, the one plane to Aalborg had just left, but then she realized it had not yet taken off. She called through to the pilot and told him I was on my way. "We'll bring him out there," she said.

The next thing I know, I'm jumping into a golf cart and some-body is driving me out across the tarmac. They opened up the door of the plane and let a ladder down so I could climb aboard. The flight was completely full, so the only free seat they had was in the cockpit with the captain and his co-pilot. The second I sat my butt down, the co-pilot looked at me and said, "Are you ready?" I said, "Yes," and *shoooom* – we took off. The flight is only about 45 minutes, and when I touched down in Aalborg, I found that Lynge had booked a car for me to the hospital. I was at my wife's bedside within little more than an hour of speaking to her mother. Everyone was shocked that I made it there so quickly, but I can only thank those great people at the airport. We never even paid for the ticket.

I was incredibly nervous about what was going to happen next because we had been trying a long time for our second baby. For some reason it wasn't happening for us, and now it seemed like we were about to lose this one. But a few moments before I arrived, the doctor had come back with some test results and told my wife everything was still OK. We'd had a scare, but the baby was fine. Jannie was not in pain, and the doctor said everything was stable.

A few hours later, I called Lynge and said, "I'm ready to go, I want to play against Lyn Oslo." Nobody on the team expected me to make the game, and they would have happily let me stay with my wife. But as long as she was OK, I was not willing to miss it. I managed to convince

Lynge that everything was alright, and he got me on a flight first thing the next morning. We tied 0-0.

I have tons of stories like that of times in my career where I refused to miss games. Most of them aren't quite so dramatic, but I have played sick, I have played hurt, and I have missed all sorts of family occasions. That's how I wound up playing 398 consecutive games for Aalborg – I hated the idea of ever being somewhere else while my team was playing. I never really thought about the record or counted the number of games until afterward. I just wanted to play soccer.

A few years earlier, when I was around twenty-five or twenty-six, I had been named as captain by Aalborg manager Erik Hamrén. That came completely out of the blue, so I asked him, "Why me?" He said I had a good training mentality and he liked the way I communicated with the rest of the team, building good relationships with everybody on the roster. That was a big compliment, so I said, "OK, why not?" It happened before the story with the bookie shutting down, but I kept the job after that, too. Despite everything I was doing wrong off the field, I must have been doing something right on it.

Since then, I have been made captain at a couple more of the clubs I went on to play for, including Sporting Kansas City. I can honestly say it's not something I've ever sought or even really thought about; I've never tried to be anyone other than my usual self. But, of course, it is a great honor to be asked, and I've always said yes.

But it wasn't true that everybody liked me. There was one spell during my wife's pregnancy where I wasn't playing very well and the Aalborg fans really started to get on my back. I know I've talked about that technique I used on the field to cut out things that might have distracted me, but for the first time, it wasn't really working. I was worried about Jannie – who wound up having to stay in the hospital for almost three months before she gave birth – and what was going to happen to our baby.

We lost at home to FC Copenhagen, 1-0, then 4-2 on the road to a team called Nordsjælland, and I made mistakes in both games. Then we came back home and lost 4-3 to Brondby, and once again I was the one to blame. I've told you before what that crowd was like at Aalborg.

I was in my 11th season with the team and had given them so many good years, but in the last 15 minutes of the Brondby game, they were booing me relentlessly every time I had the ball.

I had one teammate – actually, I don't even want to call him a teammate, he was just a player who happened to be on my team – who kept passing the ball back to me. Every time I tried to get rid of it, he would retrieve the ball and immediately turn around and kick it in my direction as if he wanted to give the fans another opportunity to boo. That was a dark moment. I don't know why he did it, and I probably never will. But at a time when my confidence was low and things were going badly, it was the last thing I needed.

The fans came back around, though. After a while, my performances improved again – I hadn't become a bad goalkeeper overnight – and for the most part, I had a great relationship with those supporters at Aalborg because they knew I was one of them.

When I was about 25 or 26, Erik Hamrén named me as Aalborg's new captain. It was a great honor, even though it was not something I had ever particularly sought. Despite all my bad decisions off the field, it was nice to think that I must have been doing something right on it.

They had nothing to do with my decision to leave the club in the summer of 2007. I was sitting at home one day when a phone call arrived out of the blue. It was from an agent asking if I might be interested in a move to Leicester City. They were an English team which played in the second-highest division, and it felt like the chance to finally put right all those wrongs from Millwall at the start of my career.

Even more importantly, it was an opportunity to finally clear my debt. We had been paying money off steadily, gradually reducing the amount I owed, but Leicester was offering me £12,500 ($18,750) per week in salary, which was far more than I could make in Denmark.

I had signed a new contract at Aalborg not long before, which had a release clause stipulating that if a foreign club bid for me and I wanted to leave, the club had to let me do so. The whole deal went through very smoothly. I spoke to Lynge, and he was never going to stand in the way of me trying to fulfill my dreams. I was twenty-nine by now and had been a good servant to Aalborg. Lynge, like most of the other people there, wanted me to be happy.

Sadly, happiness was not what I found at Leicester. Instead, I walked into a complete mess: a team with something like 50 players on the roster and which seemed to be changing managers every five minutes.

When I arrived, the man in charge was Martin Allen, and he had only been appointed that summer. The media in England used to call him 'Mad Dog' because of the way he charged all over the field in his playing days. That was the sort of mentality I liked in a player, extremely intense, but it was pretty hard for me to like him as a coach. About a week after I arrived at the club, he called me into his office and said, "I never wanted to sign you."

I was completely thrown, so I just said, "What?" He said, "You were signed by the sporting director before I got here, but I have my own goalkeeper I want to sign. I'm going to do everything I can to bring him here." That turned out to be Márton Fülöp, and he joined from Sunderland about a month after I arrived from Aalborg.

If my relationship with Allen had got off to a bad start, it was nothing compared to the one I had with the team's goalkeeping coach, Mike Stowell. He had been sacked by the club at the end of the previous season, but a few days into preseason Allen decided to bring him back in. I was happy when I heard the news because we needed a goalkeeping coach. That sense of satisfaction didn't last long.

My first meeting with Stowell was in the hallway at the team's practice facility. He was fairly young for a coach – maybe in his early forties – and he seemed friendly enough at first. He said, "Hey, aren't you the new goalkeeper?" I confirmed that I was. "I'm Mike, the new goalkeeping coach. I'm looking forward to working with you." I said, "Me too. I'll see you out there."

So I changed into my practice gear and headed out toward the field. There was a small set of steps at the back of the building that housed our locker room, and I was coming up them when I saw Stowell waiting at the top. I said, "Hey coach, what's the plan?"

"Ten push-ups."

I was confused. I hadn't even got to the field yet, and I didn't really understand what was going on. I started to speak, but he interrupted and said, "Twenty push-ups."

"What for?"

"Thirty push-ups."

Now I was getting annoyed. I told him, "You can count to a million. I'm not going to take those push-ups until you explain what the problem is. Did I do something wrong?"

He snarled back at me. "Listen, I'm in charge here. You only speak when I give you permission to speak."

All I could think was, *Are you kidding me? Is this a joke?* I wasn't some kid coming out of the academy: I was a nearly thirty-year-old man. As a soccer player, you accept that you need to listen to your coaches and do what they tell you, but that isn't a reason for them to treat you like dirt. I hadn't done anything unreasonable and would have done the push-ups if he had simply offered me some explanation as to what was going on. Instead, he kept on saying the same thing, "Get down there and take those push-ups."

"No, I'm not doing it."

He turned around and started counting all the goalkeepers who were already out on the field, pointing at each one as he went. "We have one, two, three ..." Then he deliberately looked at me, didn't count me, moved on to the next guy and continued counting. "... four, five goalkeepers at practice today. You are not involved. Go back inside and get changed."

I had been there for a few days training with those other guys before he arrived, and I couldn't believe this was happening. I refused to go in, staying on the sideline to watch instead. He marched off to start practice with the other goalkeepers, and after a few minutes I picked up one of the spare balls and started juggling it between my feet. But Stowell saw me doing that and screamed at me to stop, so I put the ball down and went inside. I was so wound up that I had to do something, so I went to the gym inside the team facility to work out.

After a few minutes, one of the assistant coaches came in and said the manager wanted to speak to me. I had a pretty good idea of how that was going to go. I walked into Martin Allen's office, and he was spitting with rage. "Are you refusing to take orders from the coach?" he demanded. I said, "No, I'm not."

"Mike told me that you refused to follow his instructions."

"That's not how it happened. He told me to do a bunch of push-ups, but when I asked him a question, he doubled the number and started adding more and more. He never told me what was going on. I only wanted to know what the plan was."

He started cursing at me. "Listen, when Mike tells you do push-ups, you don't question it. You get down there and take your push-ups. We pay your wages and you're here to do what we say."

I turned around and walked out. I wasn't interested in getting shouted at anymore by a guy who had already told me he didn't want me on his team. The next day, I received a letter telling me I had been fined a week's wages. It was Millwall all over again, except this time even worse.

The whole environment around the club was rotten. I wasn't the only person who hated Mike Stowell. He was a snake, the sort of guy who would pretend to be your friend and ask what you'd been up to the night before, and if you mentioned anything at all that could get you in trouble – like if you had stayed out at dinner until late – he would run straight to the manager and tell him everything.

He wasn't the only one, though. Allen only lasted four games as manager before getting fired, because half the coaches on his staff were out to get him. They all wanted his job for themselves. Stowell even had a few weeks as interim manager. Never in my career, before or since, have I been at a place with such a bad atmosphere. Everybody was out for himself and nobody seemed to care about what was best for the club. There was a lot of money being wasted by keeping so many players on the roster, too. I felt bad for the owner because I was sure he couldn't have known what was going on.

My family wasn't happy in Leicester, either. Our youngest daughter, Isabella, was still too young to go to school, but Mille hated the one we sent her to. I had asked before I signed if there were any international schools in the area, but there weren't, so instead we got recommended a place which claimed to have lots of experience dealing with foreign students. Maybe they had, but all I can say is that they did a terrible job of making my daughter feel welcome. Her classes were all over the school and nobody made any effort to help her integrate. She had learned some English in Denmark, but she was still only ten and had a very hard time making friends.

I used to drop her off at school every morning, but the timings didn't really work out. The school gates opened at 8.45am, and I had to be at practice at 9. It was about a 20-minute drive between the two, but I never wanted to leave Mille there on the sidewalk, waiting for somebody to open the school up, especially with her being so unhappy. She would sit crying in the back of the car as we got to the gates, and I felt like the worst dad in the world telling her she had to get out. Usually I would stay with her until there was at least somebody else there she knew, so I always wound up getting to practice five minutes late.

Arriving late to practice got me fined, and whoever the manager was at that time would get mad at me. In the end I said, "You know what? You can fine me every day if you want to, but I'm going to be five minutes late because it's more important that I look after my daughter than worrying about your stupid fines." It wasn't as if I cared what the team thought at that point. The way they had treated me, why should I?

159

You won't be surprised to hear that I collected a few more fines over the next six months. After getting off on the wrong foot with both Stowell and Allen, I got dropped straight away to the reserve team and before long they didn't even want me to start in those games. One morning, Stowell came over at the end of practice and told me he was going to try a younger goalie for the reserve team that evening. He said to take the night off and he would see me the next day at practice.

A few hours after I got home, he tried to phone me. I saw his name come up on the caller ID, but I thought, *I'm not going to spend one second on the phone with this dude.* The phone kept ringing and ringing, but I ignored it. By the end of the day, I had about 25 missed calls from him. The next day, I went in for practice and started getting changed. Stowell came running over to me and said, "What the hell is wrong with you? Why didn't you answer my calls?" I didn't say anything at first, so he kept on yelling. "Are you going to sit there and ignore me?"

"Hey, you told me I had the night off," I said. "Why should I waste any time on you if you're not going to waste any time on me?"

"I needed you to play last night, the other guy got sick and I didn't have any goalkeepers."

"That's not true. You told me on day one that you have five other goalkeepers. You should have picked one of those."

"Listen, you are supposed to be available when I need you. You have to carry your phone with you at all times."

"I had my phone on me. You called me about twenty-five times. I just chose not to answer."

He didn't know what to say to that, so he walked away, and the next day I received a letter telling me that I had been fined another week's wages – £12,500. It was pretty stupid, really, but he had set the tone on that first day. I had no respect for the man.

The next time they tried to fine me, I really hadn't done anything wrong. Stowell was serving as interim manager by this point. On the day of his first home game, he told us that the whole roster had to show up at the stadium to find out if we were on the team. I was the first guy in there. There was nobody else there yet, so I went to the player lounge and watched some TV.

After a while, I left the lounge and went to check the board where they put up the list showing who is in the team and who is on the bench. Not surprisingly, my name wasn't on it, so I walked back upstairs to the player lounge, watched the game and eventually went home.

The next morning, I was on the stationary bike in our practice facility when one of the team assistants came and handed me a letter. It said I had been fined another week's wages. There was no explanation offered. I jumped off the bike and ran after the guy who had given it to me and said, "What's this about?" but he had no idea. He said he would call Stowell to find out.

He returned a few minutes later and said, "You didn't show up at the stadium yesterday."

"Are you kidding? Didn't you see me at the stadium yesterday?"

"Yeah, I did."

"So I think you better call him back and ask what the real problem is."

"Oh, he said you didn't show up at the right time."

"I was the first damn person there. I went up to the players' lounge, watched some TV, saw the list and then went back up. I said hello to you, I said hello to everybody else I saw. Then after the game, I left."

"Sorry, there is nothing I can do."

"Right, then I'm going to have to speak to the CEO."

So I called the CEO and made an appointment to see him that afternoon. I walked into his office and threw the letter on the desk in front of him. I said, "If I'm made to pay this fine, then I can promise you right now that I will go to the newspapers and tell them about the way I've been treated at this club. I'm going to tell them how you've been cheating me."

"What do you mean, 'cheating you'?"

"Well, for starters, when I first got here you told me that you would put me in a five-star hotel until my family and I had found a place to stay. Except that when the time came to leave that hotel, nobody at the club had paid the bill, so we had to cover it ourselves."

That was true. It really wasn't the biggest of my concerns – the wages were high enough to cover the hotel cost – but I knew it was something that would make them look bad if it ever got out. He started to tell me that the team would reimburse me straight away, but I cut him off and said, "I don't care about that. This is a point of principle we're talking about now. If you try to make me pay this fine, when I was the first person in that locker room on Saturday, then I promise you I will go to the papers. I will make up lies if I have to, exactly like the person here who is trying to say that I didn't show up when I was supposed to."

Then I walked out. The next day, I got another letter telling me that the fine had been withdrawn but that I was to receive an official warning for my behavior. I'd only been at Leicester for a couple of months and already my relationship with the club was at rock bottom.

I never received a single fine in my twelve years at Aalborg, yet in England I couldn't seem to stay out of trouble. A lot of that was my own fault. Those first two fines – for refusing to do the push-ups and for ignoring Stowell's phone calls – I paid without complaint. But there is a different mentality in England. The wages are so high that some coaches get this idea that you are their property and should do whatever they say without having any opinions of your own. And maybe they're right. But no matter how much a person is getting paid, they still deserve to be treated with respect.

At a certain point, the club started trying to get rid of me. I showed up for practice one day and ran into the trainer. He said, "Oh, it's so cool to hear that you're going out on loan today. I'm so happy for you."

I had no idea what he was talking about, so I had to ask him to explain. Apparently the manager, a new guy named Frank Burrows, had told him I was going on loan to Luton Town, a team from the division below Leicester. The whole deal had already been agreed to.

"This is the first I've heard about it," I said. "But I can guarantee you I'm not going anywhere. I'm staying right here."

The stupid thing was that I didn't have any objection to the idea of joining Luton. There have been lots of times in recent years where I have thought, *Darn it, I should have gone to Luton, it could have been fun.* But the way they tried to make that move happen by arranging something behind my back and expecting me to go along with it made me so angry. They had treated me so badly from day one that I didn't want to do anything to make them happy. The trainer told me I should go and have a word with the manager, but I said that if the manager wanted to talk, he should come to me.

So once again I got called to the manager's office while halfway through getting changed. I walked over there and as soon as I got in the door, Frank Burrows said, "Hey Jim, you're going to Luton Town today on loan." We had a conversation a lot like the one I'd had with the trainer, where I told him that I wasn't going anywhere. Eventually he said, "Let's talk about it after practice."

During practice, Stowell kept telling me that I should go. I ignored him. After practice, I got called to the manager's office again, but this time it was more than Frank Burrows waiting for me. This time the manager had been joined by the CEO, the goalkeeping coach, the trainer, the fitness coach, the team administrator and a couple of others. There must have been seven or eight guys in total, all sitting in horseshoe formation and facing a single empty chair in the middle of the room. That was where I had to sit, like the accused facing the jury.

The CEO spoke first. He said, "I hear you don't want to go on loan," and I replied, "Yeah, I want to stay here and fight for my place." We all knew that was ridiculous – they had never given me a chance to do that from the day I arrived – but I said it anyway. The CEO was trying to be diplomatic, saying, "Well, I think it might be better for you to go," but I kept saying the same thing over and over.

Finally, the manager lost his cool. He slammed his hand down on a table next to his chair and started screaming at me. "You are only here for the money," he said. "You don't care about this team. You are a selfish idiot." Well, that's the censored version anyway. He kept going for about two minutes, but most of what he said I wouldn't want to print in a book that might be read by children.

When he was finished, the whole room fell silent. I waited a moment and then said, "Are you guys done?" The CEO said, "Yes. Are we agreed that you're going on loan?" I told him once again that I wasn't going anywhere, then stood up and walked out the door.

By the time I got home, I had received a text message telling me that I had been fined another week's wages and instructing me to show up the following morning at 6 for practice, three hours earlier than normal. This time I did as I was told, but when I arrived at the facility, nobody was there. I stayed in my car, waiting for someone to show up. At 7:15, Stowell arrived. "Put on your running shoes," he said. "We're going for a run."

We did that for 45 minutes, and at the end he told me to go home and return at the same time the following day. Once again, I got there at 6 in the morning and waited more than an hour for him to arrive. And when he did, we went for another run. This carried on for a few days, though after the first time I always came a bit better prepared. I brought a newspaper to read in the car as well as a coffee and some breakfast.

After a few days, at the end of our run, I told Stowell, "This really isn't a punishment for me; I love training. Running isn't my favorite thing in the world, but I like to work out and get fit. I also have a kid who wakes up at 5 every morning, so this is a nice bit of peace and quiet for me."

Two days after that conversation, I received a text telling me not to come to practice any more. That was on a Sunday, so the following day I stayed home. But on Tuesday morning there was another letter in my mailbox, telling me that I had been fined for not showing up to practice. There was no stamp on the envelope, so they must have sent someone round first thing to drop it off by hand. We lived right across the road from the stadium, so I marched over there, straight into the CEO's office. I showed him both the letter and the text, and for the second time he was forced to retract a fine that the coaches had tried to give me.

They continued to freeze me out of practice until a few weeks later, when I got another text message saying that the team would appreciate it if I tried to find another club during the January transfer window. I sent one back which read: "Nobody is interested in Leicester City's No. 7 goalkeeper."

Maybe that message struck a chord, or maybe they realized they had no hope of getting me to leave without my consent, because after that, the communication between me and the CEO seemed to become a bit more respectful. We had a few good conversations, and we tried to find a solution that worked for both of us. I was costing them a lot of money to not even sit on the bench, and I didn't really want to be there, but there really weren't any teams lining up to sign me.

In the end, he agreed to buy me out of my contract. I don't remember exactly what fee we settled on, though it was less than I would have got in wages if I had stayed through the duration of the deal but enough to clear off almost all of my remaining debt. After all the bad financial decisions I made in my younger life, I owed my family that. I knew there was a good chance I was never going to get a

I don't have many happy memories of Leicester, but this was one of the few. On Halloween, we invited my teammate Adda Djeziri (who was also Danish) round for dinner, and everybody was in fancy dress. Adda's costume was the real showstopper – he's the one on the left – but I thought I made a pretty good angel, too. After dinner, Adda and I went to pick up some dessert from a nearby restaurant. That was a weird experience. People were very polite when we walked in, but we heard the whole restaurant explode with laughter the second we walked out.

contract like this one again, and I couldn't walk away from it without getting compensated.

So that was the end of my second English adventure. It had lasted all of half a season. Once again I was heading back to Denmark. After a second failed move away from the country of my birth, I was beginning to think that maybe the grass really wasn't greener on the other side.

17
FALLING OUT OF LOVE

Aalborg had signed a replacement goalkeeper after I left in the summer of 2007, Karim Zaza, and he was doing very well, so there was no chance for me to return there after leaving Leicester. In any case, I'm not sure it would have been the right move. I had left in the hope of trying something different, and even if I was now heading back to Denmark, it was still time for me to take on a new challenge.

There was a team called Vejle, which was playing in the second division of Danish soccer at that time but which was historically a very successful club. It had been champion of Denmark four times in the 1970s and 1980s, and after a barren period, it was now trying to build a new team. The season was already halfway through, but Vejle was on course for promotion and had invested a lot of money in new players.

Vejle also had a coach named Ove Christensen, whom I had never worked with before but who used to live very near me in Aalborg. We would work out at the same gym in our city during the off-season, so we ran into each other there all the time. He was a good coach who had worked for a few different clubs in Denmark – usually ones that were overachieving on small budgets – and I admired his work a lot. I also knew we got along well, which was important after everything that had happened in England.

As soon as it became clear that I was leaving Leicester, I put out a few phone calls to different people back home to see what opportunities might be out there. Ove got in touch and it didn't take us long to work out a deal. We had already agreed to the terms before Leicester released me, and the day after they did, I traveled to Vejle to sign the contract.

At first we moved back to Aalborg, which was about a two-hour drive from Vejle, since that would allow Mille to go back to her old school as well as putting us close to our families. But after a year, the commute to practice had become a bit much, so we moved to Vejle. It was a nice place, slightly smaller than Aalborg and with a population of about 100,000, but it was otherwise pretty similar. It was another soccer-obsessed city where everybody knew exactly what was going on with the team and the city's mood would go up or down depending on how we did.

Vejle already had a goalkeeper, Jan Hoffman, when I arrived, but he was always planning to retire at the end of the season, so he decided to step aside and bring that forward by a few months. I went straight into the team as his replacement, and we had a fun end to the season. We were the best team in the division by a long way, and we set a new record for the most points ever recorded by a team in a single season at that level: 78 out of a possible 90.

Not long after I arrived, Vejle also opened up a brand new stadium. We had been using this very old-fashioned and run-down building where they had played for many years, but a month or two before the end of the season, they completed work on the replacement and we moved in. It wasn't especially big – room for maybe 11,000 people – but it had this very close, intense atmosphere which made it super-cool to play in.

So I was having a lot of fun. It was nice to feel like I was back with a club that wanted me around. Not long after I arrived, Christensen made me the captain. But more important was the simple fact that I got to play a game every week.

The mood turned quickly after we were promoted, though. The team's directors signed a whole bunch of players, many of whom were very talented but whose arrival damaged the team chemistry. Some of the guys who had worked to get the team promoted resented the new players coming in and taking their jobs. The locker room became divided, with everybody clinging to their little groups of friends and not trusting anybody else. I like to think that as captain I got along with everybody, but even if they would all talk to me, I couldn't always get them to speak to each other.

I kept saying, "Look, you don't have to be friends, but when we step out onto the field, you need to be teammates." The general manager even hired a psychologist to help work with us on the mental side of things, but that didn't help. The real problem was that we kept losing. Very often in soccer you find these problems can just disappear when you start winning games. But when you're losing every week, it reinforces all the negative thoughts people are having.

The directors also made a poor decision, in my opinion, to fire Coach Christensen. It was right after the winter break and we were bottom of the league, but I truly believe he would have kept us in the division. I know I will never be able to prove that one way or another, but we had been playing our best football of the season, and even though we weren't getting the results we deserved, I am convinced that we could have turned things around with him in charge.

Vejle knew I wouldn't be happy they had fired him. The general manager called me up on the morning of the announcement as I was dropping Isabella off at daycare. He asked me to come into his office,

Before each season, Vejle held a big fan rally. As the captain, I got to announce the roster for the coming season at that event. It was a big deal, especially the year after we got promoted. We took over a whole shopping mall and 1,000 fans came down to hang out with us players and get their jerseys signed. Not a bad turnout for a city of 100,000 people.

where he explained the decision to me. I knew it wouldn't change anything, but I told him immediately that it was the wrong thing to do. They didn't appoint a new manager for the rest of the season; they simply handed over duties on an interim basis to the academy coach, Lasse Christensen, and an assistant named Ole Schwennesen.

The season continued to slip away from us. We had drawn all of our last three games under Ove Christensen, 1-1, and in two of those we had taken the lead first. About three weeks after he left, we had a home game against FC Midtjylland, which was a good team in the top half of the table. We were up 2-0 after 58 minutes but wound up losing 3-2. They scored in the 63rd, 75th and 77th minutes. I think that game really broke us.

I'd had a big miscommunication with one of our defenders on their tying goal. I ran out of my penalty area to try to clear a ball, but my teammate was going for it at the same time. I told him to leave it for me, but he obviously didn't hear, because he tried to pass it to me. The ball went straight by me, and so did one of their attackers, who slotted the ball into the empty net.

Ove Christensen, the man without glasses in the middle of this picture, was the manager at Vejle when I arrived, and he played a big role in my decision to join the club. He led us to promotion into the Danish Superliga – the top division – but then got fired halfway through my second season with the club. I will always believe that was a poor decision by Vejle. He was a fantastic coach.

That's the way things go when you're losing games. You start to feel like you can't catch a break, and it begins to affect your confidence, which only makes things worse. For a long time it felt like our opponents had more players than we did. It could be 11 against 11 on the field, but if I was standing in my goal and the opponents were playing in yellow, I would look up and see nothing but yellow jerseys. It was like our guys had become invisible. I felt constantly overwhelmed.

We weren't relegated until the second-last game of the season. It wasn't an especially memorable game, a 1-0 defeat to Randers, but it was typical of how we were playing then. No confidence, no inspiration. From the opening kickoff, we played like a beaten team. It was a horrible, horrible feeling when the final whistle blew. Nobody was shocked that we had been relegated. We had been at the bottom of the table for the whole season, but you always kept hoping for a miracle. The miracle never arrived.

Personally, I was still ready to give it another shot in the lower division. I'm a competitive guy, and the first thing I thought after getting relegated was, *OK, we'll start again and get back up like we did last time.* But Vejle hired a new manager in the offseason, and we didn't hit it off.

He was a Swedish coach named Mats Gren, and from day one he seemed more interested in my body fat percentage than how I was performing on the field. I won't pretend I was the leanest guy on the team, but all through my career I had always made sure I was in good enough shape to play soccer. If my weight had ever affected my performance, I would have addressed it, but as long as I was playing well, I didn't see why it should be an issue. Let's not forget my hero growing up was Neville Southall, who managed to be a great goalkeeper despite being a lot bigger than I ever was.

Gren wanted the measurements every day: how much did I weigh and how much of that was muscle. He told me I had to come in an hour earlier than everyone else and ride a bike before practice, then stay late to do the same thing again at the end of the day. That's all he was interested in – not whether I had made any great saves in practice or had done well controlling my area and claiming crosses. All he wanted to know was how much I had exercised.

For the first time in my whole life, I stopped enjoying soccer. I had gone through some miserable spells at Millwall and Leicester, but those were very different. At Millwall, I was unhappy with the lack of instruction at practice and the loneliness of life off the field, but I was still desperate to get a game every weekend. At Leicester, I hated the goalkeeping coach and the way the club treated me. But the thing that upset me most was never getting to play.

It wasn't like that at Vejle. The team wasn't fining me and trying to force me out the door like they had at Leicester. But Gren sucked all of the joy out of soccer and turned it from a game I loved into something much less fun. Instead of tactics and skills, all we ever seemed to work on was fitness, fitness, fitness. It made me not want to go to work in the morning, and even the fact I'm calling it 'work' gives you some indication of how my mindset changed. Soccer wasn't fun any longer. It was a job – a boring, shitty job.

It became clear pretty quickly that we weren't going to bounce straight back up to the top division. We had good enough players, but between the divisions in the locker room and Gren's poor leadership, we couldn't reach the levels we were capable of. We were stuck in mid-table by the winter break, and the team started selling off and cutting players to bring the wage bill down.

Toward the end of January, three or four days before the transfer window was set to close, I got a phone call from a reporter at *Tipsbladet*, the big sports magazine where I used to get my betting tips. He was a guy I had spoken to plenty of times who wanted to ask a few questions, so I didn't mind talking. I answered him very professionally, saying only things I knew the team would be happy with.

But then he cut to the chase and asked, "How do you see your future with this team? Do you imagine yourself having a long-term future at Vejle?"

I was quiet for a few seconds, thinking about how to come up with a diplomatic answer. And then I decided to tell him the truth. "I don't see myself having any future with this team," I said. "I'm not enjoying my soccer here, and I need to find a new place."

The magazine came out the next day. I had just dropped the kids off at school and was driving past a shop. I looked up at the window and saw my own face staring back at me – they had put the piece about me on the front page. I always knew they were going to make a story out of what I said, but I honestly didn't realize what a big deal it would be.

I thought, *Oh God*, but I also knew I hadn't said anything I didn't mean. What was the point in lying to protect a job I hated? I didn't know what else to do, so I showed up for practice as usual and went straight to the locker room to start changing. The assistant came in and said, "You probably don't need to worry about putting on your practice gear. The coach wants to see you in his office."

Predictably, I got suspended from practice, but a day later Coach Gren called me back in and said that if I took back what I had said to the media, they would allow me to return. I told him I couldn't do that because it would be a lie. After a few more days he told me to come back to practice anyway, but at that point I knew this had to be the end. I returned, but I said I would only train with the academy until we found a way to resolve my situation.

I had reached the point where retiring from soccer altogether seemed more appealing than carrying on as we were. I was thirty-two, not too old for a goalkeeper, but I didn't see the point in dragging my career out any longer if I wasn't enjoying it. When you wake up every morning and immediately start thinking about whether to phone in sick, then you're not in the right place.

This wasn't some passing thought. I spent a lot of time going through the different options in my head, thinking about what I could do next and how our family would get by. We still had a bit of the money from Leicester left over, so I had some breathing room. If another opportunity hadn't arisen at that moment, I sincerely believe I would have walked away and my soccer career would have been over.

Thankfully, something did come along, something I would never have expected in a million years: a phone call from the other side of the planet.

18
A PHONE CALL FROM OUT OF THE BLUE

I've never been a big believer in long-term plans. That's partly just a reflection of my character; I'm an impulsive guy. But it's also because, in my experience, life tends to throw you opportunities when you least expect them and for reasons you could not possibly have imagined.

Who could ever have guessed, for instance, that my career would be saved by a meaningless training ground scuffle? The incident took place in May 2009, shortly before I was relegated with Vejle and long before my interview with *Tipsbladet*. We were playing a short-sided game in practice and one of the players on the other team, a midfielder named Valentino Lai, was getting a bit carried away. I'm a big believer in giving 100% in practice and treating every game like it's a competitive one, but he was making challenges that were going to get somebody hurt. Nobody needed that. Our season was going badly enough already.

We had a little break to grab some water, and I told him, "You need to relax a little bit, those are your teammates." Then, a few moments after the restart, he came racing toward our goal, chasing a through-ball. I slid in to tackle him, probably a little bit hard, but I won the ball without even touching him. Two seconds later, he ran past me and kicked me on the back of the heel. It was nothing too violent, just a tap, but it was definitely intentional. You can see on the video that he pauses for a second to give himself the chance to do it.

At that point I lost my mind a little bit, chasing him up the pitch and giving him a shove. He turned around and pushed me back, and we quickly started trying to hit each other. But neither of us really got a chance because our teammates all jumped on us and pulled us apart.

It was a meaningless incident, the sort of thing that happens at least a couple times per season on every team I've played for. It probably happened a bit more often at Vejle, which had that tension between the original group of players and the ones who were signed after we were promoted. But I've seen lots of similar incidents on teams that are doing well. When you have a group of competitive guys together playing a sport, sooner or later things are going to go a bit further than they should. But there was no big problem between Valentino and myself. He refused to shake my hand at the end of practice because he was still wound up, but he did the next day, and between him and me, it was all forgotten.

Or at least it would have been were it not for the internet blogger standing with a camera on the sideline. He had filmed the whole thing, and when he got home afterward, he called up one of the national TV networks and sold the footage to them for their evening sports bulletin.

I had gone out for dinner that night with my wife and the two girls, visiting a friend of ours who worked in the office for Vejle. We were sitting on the couch together after our meal, watching TV, when, *boom*, there I am shoving Valentino. The voice-over was making it out to be a much bigger fight than it really was.

My phone was on fire. On. Fire. I went outside to answer the first few calls, but every time I hung up it started ringing again straight away. After a while, I left my phone in the car and went back inside so as not to ruin the rest of our evening. When we came back out a few hours later, I had close to 100 missed calls. The national news sent a TV camera down to our practice the next day and for several more afterward. They never saw anything more exciting than the handshake.

The media in Denmark is very negative. People only ever seem to be interested in bad stories, and the reporters are always more interested in a negative angle than a positive one. That's not only in soccer. Any time somebody in the country starts doing well in business or any other area of life, it feels like the media starts searching straight away to see if it can find out something bad about the person. I actually felt like I had a good relationship with most of the reporters I used to speak to, despite all the bad headlines I had made in my career. But I never liked that approach of always wanting a bad story rather than a good one.

In the end, though, the video turned out to be one of the best things that ever happened to me. A few months later, all the way across the Atlantic Ocean, a group of Kansas City Wizards coaches were watching film of a bunch of different goalkeepers, and they stumbled across that video. I guess they saw something they liked because not long after seeing it, the manager, Peter Vermes, gave me a call.

I had been sitting at home one afternoon when I got a text from a number I didn't recognize. The message said it was from an agent I'd never heard of, asking whether I might be interested in playing for Kansas City. Everybody in Denmark knew about my situation after the article in *Tipsbladet*, and there are a lot of agents who do business in an opportunistic way by responding to stories in the papers, so it wasn't a huge shock to get such a message. I texted him back saying yes and asking when I might hear more. He replied, saying, "Their manager is going to phone you in the next two minutes."

This I wasn't expecting. I'd had plenty of messages and phone calls from agents down the years, but normally they were just sounding me out, trying their luck with me before going back to the team. Most of the time they would ask me one question, I would reply, and then I would never hear from them again. This was different. My phone rang two minutes later, as the agent had promised.

I had thought about retiring so often by this point that I was beginning to come to terms with the idea. I answered the call as much out of curiosity as anything else. But I can tell you now that if Peter Vermes had been my manager at Vejle, I would never have even thought about quitting soccer. Over the next hour, we shared one of the most exciting and motivational conversations of my entire life. By the time we were finished, I wanted to run out to the nearest park and play soccer with anybody who happened to be around.

Peter had only become the coach of Kansas City during the previous season, and although it had finished near the bottom of the standings, he had big plans about building something great. He told me about the team, his vision for how it could get bigger, and how soccer was growing in America. He told me about Kansas City itself and what a great place it was to live, but I was barely even listening. All I could think was, *Jesus Christ! I want to play for this guy.*

I told Peter as much before we got off the phone, and a few minutes later he sent me an email with an offer on it. Again, I barely read it. I sent him a message back saying that, as long as we could reach an agreement with Vejle, I was in. I hadn't even spoken to my family yet; in fact, I didn't even know where Kansas City was. I had to call Peter back and get him to give me directions while I looked for it on a map.

There were things I guess he didn't know about me, either, because he phoned me the next day with a few questions about my gambling problem. I was completely honest with him, telling him what had happened but also explaining it had been several years since I had last placed a bet. I said if he wanted to add anything into the contract about gambling, then I was happy for him to do so, but he replied that he trusted me.

The other thing I hadn't done was ask him about Kansas City's existing goalkeeper situation. When I finally went to look on the team's website, I found out they already had a guy named Kevin Hartman, who had been the starter for three years, was part of the national team, and held the league record for most saves. I was wondering, *What on Earth do they need me for?* Then an even worse thought hit: *This is going to be exactly like Leicester City.*

I phoned Peter and asked him why he needed a goalkeeper. These are questions I probably should have asked the first time round, but like I say, I was too excited. In any case, he put my mind at ease, explaining Kevin was about to leave. That was a big relief. He hadn't told me I was guaranteed to be the starter – nor would I expect him to – but I wanted to believe I at least had a shot at it.

Peter's phone call arrived in February 2010, and a few days later I was off to Kansas City. Vejle was struggling financially, so it wasn't hard to persuade the team to release me from my contract. I paid a little bit of money, and I believe Kansas City paid a bit of money, too. I was lucky to have an understanding family, which was happy to join me on this new adventure. They had to do all the packing because

Sporting KC had already begun their preseason, so I flew out straight away and left Jannie in charge. She was awesome, as always.

As I sat on the plane, waiting to fly to America, I wasn't nervous or anxious, just simply excited to try something new. I had never even watched a Major League Soccer game before, but I felt like I had nothing to lose. I was ready to quit the sport altogether beforehand, so it could hardly be much worse than life at Vejle. My contract, like most in MLS, was also only for one year, so if it turned out to be a disaster, I wouldn't have to stick it out very long. Even if we made it to the playoffs, the season would be over by mid-November.

Everybody can survive nine months, I thought. *How bad can it be?*

I suppose a little part of me also wondered what had convinced Peter Vermes to sign a goalkeeper he had never met. Rather than guess, I'll let him talk you through it…

We had been discussing a new contract with Kevin Hartman and his agent for a very long time, and I think it was twenty-seven days into preseason when I finally said, "I've had enough," and decided to look into some different options. The only problem is that once you're that close to the season, you start having to make decisions very quickly.

Between me and my staff, we have a lot of connections across the footballing world, so we contacted various people we knew for suggestions of goalkeepers who might be available and of the quality we were looking for. Sometimes we're proactive in looking for players – there will be someone we've noticed during games we've seen – but on this occasion, Jimmy was presented to us, and we set about trying to find out as much as we could about him in a short space of time.

Typically when we are looking at a foreign player, we will watch him on video and on the internet, but we also always have to go and see him live at least once. That's the absolute minimum. Unfortunately, in this situation we didn't have that luxury. It was a big risk – goalkeeper is a very important position – but we watched a lot of tape on Jimmy and thought he was a good player. Then we found the video of him getting into a fight in practice. I loved it, as did our goalkeeping coach, John Pascarella.

I was a pretty intense player myself, and as much as I believe in the team concept, I don't think it means you need to be afraid of strong personalities. A lot of managers are afraid of intense players because they think those personalities will be a distraction for their team or will be hard to coach. For me, it's the exact opposite. This business is tough. You're evaluated every week for what you do on the field, and you're constantly under the microscope. If you're weak, then when things go badly, you're going to break. If you're strong, you'll bend and then come back.

The video showed me that Jimmy was competitive, that he wasn't going to take any crap. But it wasn't like that was my only impression of him. I'd spoken to a lot of people in Denmark besides Jimmy – people who knew the game – and they all told me he had a background of being a team guy. So that fire he showed in the video was simply one component of his character.

I decided to get Jimmy on the phone. I always speak to players personally to get a feel for who they are and what they're about. As soon as my conversation with Jimmy was done, I told my staff straight away, "I've got a great connection with this guy." I liked his personality. The things I didn't know about were his fitness and his readiness to play.

I remember the conversation because it was very similar to the one I have with all foreign players coming in. I've had the luxury of being a foreign player myself in a few different countries, and I've also had the experience of both playing and coaching at home in Major League Soccer, seeing foreign players coming into the league. On top of that, I was the technical director and general manager of this team before I became manager in 2009 and took responsibility for all of those roles together. So I think I have a lot of good experience, and I've used it to create a list of questions and statements I put to every foreign player.

My first questions are: "Are you still motivated to play this game, and do you have a lot left to prove as a player?" And look, a player could lie and try to pull one over on me when I ask him questions like that. But without going into all the details, I have a set of follow-up questions where I feel confident that somewhere along the line, somebody who is lying will eventually slip up. Once I got into the conversation with

Jimmy, I really believed he wasn't done yet, that he hadn't achieved everything he wanted to in his career.

The other thing I want to know is whether the player knows about our league. They don't have to know a lot about it, but what I'm interested in is whether they are going to come here with negative preconceptions.

If you could take all the foreign players who have ever come to play in MLS and formulate some measuring system by which to evaluate what would constitute success for each of them in our league, I think it's safe to say 7 out of 10 would have failed. The reason is that a lot of players come here with the mentality of: *When I get to America, it's going to be easy. The standard of soccer is not very good there.* Then they get here and they're taken aback because it's much higher than they expected. What you find out at that point is whether they have a strong enough mentality to step up or if they're going to just coast along. The ones who try to do that get found out.

That was a big part of my conversation with Jimmy: explaining to him that it was a very difficult league to play in but that if he showed up with the right mentality, he was going to be a success. And to support that, I told him a little bit about our plans to turn the team into one of the most successful and prominent in the country. We didn't even have our own soccer-specific stadium yet, but that was on the way. I knew we had an ambitious ownership group and big things were coming.

I think that was the bit that struck a chord with Jimmy. It seemed like when I started talking about a project and building something together, he wasn't pretending to listen like some players might. He was getting excited and asking questions. His reaction made me believe that if we signed him, he wasn't just going to come along for the ride – he wanted to be part of something bigger and to work to make it happen.

In my business, you have to go with your instincts sometimes, and I think we had the contract done inside twelve hours. I had heard about the gambling in Jimmy's past, and I had to ask him about it because I needed to protect our team. But for me, the questions were very simple. I asked, "Are you over it?" and, "Is this going to be a distraction for our team?" He told me he was and it wouldn't. Like I say, I had a pretty good feel for the guy after the first conversation, so that was all I needed to know.

I got asked about it at the press conference when we announced Jimmy's signing, and because he had given me such a clear answer, I was able to do the same. There were no more questions on the matter because we'd addressed it so directly. Three years later, I don't think anyone could disagree that we made the right decision.

Me and 'the gaffer': Peter Vermes. It only took me a few minutes on the phone with Peter to know that he was somebody I wanted to work for. He is a fantastic coach and an unbelievably hard-working guy who makes you want to put in the extra hours because you know he and his staff will always do the same.

19
WELCOME TO KANSAS CITY

The first time I saw the Kansas City Wizards' stadium, I thought it was the training ground. We were sharing a facility with the minor league baseball team called the T-Bones, so there was just a temporary soccer pitch set up in the outfield. My English was a little rusty, but even after someone managed to explain that this was where we played our home games, I still wasn't sure whether to believe them. I couldn't tell if it was a joke.

You got used to it, though, and the team did get the most out of it. The shape of a baseball stadium is different from what you would normally have for soccer, so they had to put additional seating up, which made the field short and narrow. Because the T-Bones were using the

The Kansas City T-Bones' stadium, where we played all our games in my first year with Sporting KC. When I first got shown around, I thought it was the practice facility.

stadium at the same time, our field also had to be temporary — they would remove it and reinstall it in between games. It was surprisingly good to play on, though. The groundskeepers were some of the best I've ever been around, and the field at our real practice facility was amazing, too.

Peter Vermes had told me a new stadium was being built, but I didn't really have a good feel for how long that was going to take or how long I was going to be around. To be honest, it wasn't my biggest concern. It was a shock to see the stadium we were playing in, but it didn't affect how I felt about joining the team. What I really wanted to know was what practice would be like.

From day one, I was blown away. I got down to the practice facility (which was very impressive), and I was introduced to all my new teammates. They seemed friendly, but I must admit I didn't have high expectations for the level of soccer. Nobody back in Denmark really watched Major League Soccer, and the assumptions were mostly negative. Peter warned me when we first spoke that it would be tougher than I expected, but I was still surprised.

A few people in Denmark had joked with me about MLS being a retirement league and how I could put my feet up, but I could see straight away that those guys didn't know what they were talking about. The style of soccer in the US is different, the tactics and the way people approach the game is not the same, but the standard is at least as high as in Denmark, if not better.

The players' attitudes to training were unbelievable. You might remember that there was a guy at Aalborg named Søren Thorst, who I used to admire growing up because of the way he gave 100% commitment every time he stepped on the field. Here it was like we had a whole roster full of players with the exact same spirit.

I had never been on a team like it. In Europe, there are always some guys playing more for the fame or the money than their love of soccer. You can always tell those players in practice; they are the ones saying, "Oh, I'm too tired today" or sitting out because they feel a little sore. In Kansas City, there was nobody like that – practice was relentless every single day.

It's impossible for me to say whether that's an American trait or something specific to our team. I do know that the coaching in Kansas City set a tone. Peter Vermes was every bit as motivating in real life as he had been on the phone. He demands an incredible amount from people, but he does the same with himself. He's out there at 6:00 a.m. every day before practice, and he can stay at the facility until midnight. When he asks you to work hard, you listen because you know he is doing the same.

Peter also has this unwavering belief in what he does. The few times later down the line, when results turned against us and things weren't going our way, he never changed course. You will see a lot of coaches who start to doubt themselves in that situation and take their foot off the gas pedal for a moment, altering practice to make it more lighthearted and telling the players to take a break. Peter doesn't do any of those things because he is so certain he's doing the right thing. He comes in full of energy every day and transmits that to the players. He's also very clear in the way he communicates, telling us exactly what he wants.

The goalkeeping coach, John Pascarella, is exactly the same way. He was unbelievable right from my first practice, bringing back the motivation and excitement for soccer I thought I had lost. For me,

Photo courtesy of Gary Rohman

From my very first training session in Kansas City, I knew I was going to get along with our goalkeeping coach, John Pascarella. He is such a positive guy to be around, someone who knows how to crack a joke and make everybody smile, while running an extremely professional and effective practice session at the same time. He is the best in America at what he does.

soccer should be fun – it's important to be able to laugh sometimes, but you also have to be serious about quality. John was very good at knowing when to break the tension with a joke, and you understood as a player when you could do so as well. But you also knew when it was time to get to work.

Within a few days I had completely forgotten about Denmark and how things finished at Vejle, because John gave me so much energy. He is an unbelievably positive guy, one who always tries to find the best in every situation. Every morning you look forward to working with John because you know he will be there with a big smile on his face. I love that attitude. I like to think I have a similar mindset, but between the years of debt and those difficult times at Leicester and Vejle, I had lost it for a little while. Now it came flooding back.

After my first day of practice, I called home, so excited. Jannie and the girls weren't supposed to be coming out to join me for another month or so, but I told them, "You've got to get over here quicker, it's awesome." I hadn't found anywhere for us to live yet, but I knew we'd work something out. So I moved their flights forward by a fortnight, and we lived in a hotel room for the first few weeks after they arrived. They were every bit as excited as me, and they loved it.

Our enthusiasm had a lot to do with how people were off the field. Kansas City is such a welcoming place — people here are ridiculously friendly. Right away, we had total strangers inviting us round for dinner and offering to lend us anything we might need. You could meet someone once for twenty minutes and afterward they would treat you like an old friend.

The room we were staying in at the hotel had a little kitchenette with a microwave and a fridge – enough that you could make your breakfast in the morning – so one afternoon, Jannie and I took the rental car and went out to do some grocery shopping. We went to the supermarket and picked up a few bits and pieces like soda, water and cereal, and as we were walking out to the car, the bottom split on one of our bags and everything came rolling out across the parking lot.

I bent over to start gathering it up, but when I looked up again, there were four or five people all helping us. Not staff at the supermarket, but people who happened to be there doing their shopping. Jannie and I looked at each other like, *What the hell is going on here?* If the same thing had happened in Denmark, everybody would have walked on past and pretended they didn't see anything. Not that people are rude in Denmark, but everybody is too busy worrying about their own business and what they have to do that day. The attitude was different in Kansas City, and everybody wanted to go out of their way to help you.

It was a cool moment. In the car afterward, we were both saying "Wow, people are helpful," and talking about how impressed we were. For a little while we assumed it was only because we were new and the novelty would wear off, but three years later, I'm still blown away by how welcoming the people in this city are.

A bit like with the soccer, we probably had a few negative expectations about life in America. Jannie and I both liked America and had visited before (not only to Vegas!), and we knew there were lots of things we loved, but the media back home like to sell you this image of Americans eating nothing but fast food and having terrible health. That turned out to be false. Of course, some people do eat too

Our first home in Kansas City: a small hotel room in the center of the city. We were there for a few weeks and it really wasn't ideal, but we made the best of it. This is me and my youngest daughter, Isabella, waiting for our turn in the bathroom.

much and that's sad, but the United States is such a big country with so many people in it. We can't all be the same. There are lots of great places to eat here if you want, and the grocery stores have fantastic fresh produce and meat. The fast food culture is a very small part of the overall picture.

After all those years in Denmark and England, it was a little strange coming to a place where soccer wasn't the top sport, though it didn't come as a surprise. I knew all about the NBA, the NHL and MLB, and I'm actually a big fan of the NFL. I probably shouldn't admit this as a guy who plays in Kansas City, but my favorite team was always the St. Louis Rams. They started to show the NFL on TV in Denmark in the late 1990s, right when the Rams were killing it with Kurt Warner and the Greatest Show on Turf. I loved watching him at quarterback, and I really liked their uniforms, too, the ones with the gold pants.

Football — or American football, as we called it — is a surprisingly popular sport in Denmark, and I know a lot of people who used to stay up all night to watch it. The time difference meant some games didn't finish until five in the morning, but I used to have friends over to watch games sometimes. I always thought Danish TV did a good job with their coverage. Instead of cutting to commercial breaks, a lot of the time they would go back to a studio to talk about what had happened on a certain play and explain the rules a bit better, which was good for people like me who were still learning about the sport.

So I was excited to go see a game live when I got to Kansas City. The first one I saw was between the hometown Chiefs and the San Diego Chargers at Arrowhead Stadium on a Monday night. Kansas City won 21-24. Unfortunately, they haven't won a lot of games lately, but I root for the Chiefs as well as the Rams these days. I had Chiefs season tickets in 2011, and I will get them again, as long as their schedule doesn't clash too much with ours.

I didn't mind soccer having a lower profile, either. I've never played for the fame or the attention, and I think my family was happy to have me to themselves when we went out to a restaurant or the mall. I don't mind people coming up to say hello, but there was a time back in Aalborg, after the incident with the bookie, where people would see me in public and say things that were extremely rude, even if I was there with my wife and my kids. It could be a little bit like that if results weren't going our way, too. I never reacted, but sometimes Jannie wanted to. Usually I managed to convince her that it wasn't worth it.

Most importantly, the soccer was going well. It was a bit of a shock at first to see what good shape all the players were in and how hard they were working, but I got into the swing of things. I've never been the fittest guy on any of the teams I've played for, and by the time I came to America, I definitely wasn't in top condition. My last manager at Vejle, Mats Gren, had put all that effort into trying to make me lose weight, but by stopping me from enjoying my soccer, he actually had the opposite effect: making me give up altogether.

In Kansas City, it was different. All the players were working hard because the style of soccer here demands it and because the game is played at a much higher tempo and with an aggressive, physical style. As a goalkeeper, you don't need to be fit like all the outfield players, but

I can't explain this picture, but it does make me laugh. I'm sitting on the statue of a bull outside Jack Stack Barbeque in Kansas City's Country Club Plaza. My family and I love that part of town because there are so many great places to eat and shop, but I have no idea why I got up on that bull.

seeing how much work they were doing made me want to do the same. We were all part of the team and were working our hardest to pull in the same direction.

I had to adapt my techniques, too. The goalkeeping coach, John Pascarella, only had a very short time to work with me before the season started, but he did a fantastic job of getting me ready. We watched a ton of film on different opponents, and during practice he talked me through a few adjustments he thought would help me to deal with the different style of soccer.

He was very observant — noticing little things I did on the field, then coming over and saying, "This thing might have worked for you in Europe, but the forwards act differently over here, so why don't you try this instead?" Most of it was to do with how I positioned myself in the goal. I don't want to go into specifics because you never know if an opponent might read this one day! But he gave me a few tips about the tendencies of players over here, and all I can say is it was definitely good advice.

The team's goalkeeping situation was a mess when I arrived. Well, maybe mess isn't the right word, but it was certainly a big challenge for the coaches, in that we were only a few weeks out from the season and they hadn't worked out the order at all — who was going to be No. 1, No. 2, and No. 3. They had spent money to get me in, but they didn't really know me.

I was desperate not to let them down. The team had done so much to make my life easier with the move, including arranging visas for me and my family, helping us set up an American bank account, driving us around to see different neighborhoods and look at apartments. Between all that and the fantastic coaching I was getting, I felt like I owed it to them to do well and show that they had made the right decision in signing me. I wanted Kansas City to know it had its goalkeeper and it didn't need to worry about that anymore.

There were a lot of other players going through a similar experience. The competition for places on the roster was more intense than I was used to because almost all Major League Soccer contracts only run for one year at a time. In Europe, most players are on multi-year deals, which give them a bit more certainty about where they will be playing from one season to the next. It was a year of particularly high turnover for Kansas City, so when I arrived, there were about thirty new players plus all the returning ones fighting for twenty-six spots on the roster. It was intense.

By the beginning of the season, though, I had been named as the starter. Our first game was at home against D.C. United. It was the end of March and the weather was terrible. It was freezing cold, with heavy rain and wind so hard that the water was hitting you sideways. I remember going out onto the field for the national anthem. All I could think through the whole song was: *I'm not wearing enough clothes!* Back in Denmark, I had played a million games where it was freezing cold, but I always knew how to dress properly to make sure I stayed warm.

I had to make one pretty good save after about 4 minutes. Our defender, Matt Besler, lost the ball, and one of their players passed it to Jaime Moreno on the edge of the box. He had a shot that was curling into the corner, but I managed to push it away. Of course, you'd rather not give up any chances at all, but that was a good way for me to start. I was defending the goal in front of our loudest fans, and I'm sure they were all nervous to see this guy who was replacing Kevin Hartman. I felt like they accepted me quickly after seeing that save.

We won the game 4-0, and I made a couple more saves along the way. It didn't get any warmer, though! I'm very superstitious with my routines around a game, so I couldn't change my clothes at halftime, especially not after making a good save right at the start.

I have a lot of superstitions. I need to take a nap before every game, so if we have an early kickoff, I have to move my whole day's routine forward, getting up and having my breakfast before sunrise so I can still have time to nap later on. It doesn't need to be long, 30 minutes is fine, and it can be at home or in the team hotel – wherever, so long as I get my nap.

If we're playing at home, I always eat the same food the night before the game, too. Unfortunately, I can't always control such things if we're on the road, but for the last fifteen years, I've always eaten Jannie's spaghetti with meat sauce before every home game. She has her special way of making it, and that's what I need. Every now and then the schedule will fall in such a way that the team plays three home games in a week, and though kids get absolutely sick and tired of spaghetti, I cannot change my routine. Plus, the sauce is awesome. Mille and Isabella might get bored, but I could eat it every day.

Anyway, I was happy to be off to a good start. I think a few of my teammates were a little surprised by my approach on the field. When they heard the team was signing me, a lot of them had gone online and watched the video of me getting into a fight with Valentino during practice at Vejle. They were all saying to each other, "Who is this jerk coming over?" They assumed I was going to be one of those goalkeepers who screams and shouts at his defenders whenever they make a mistake, but that has never really been my style.

Don't get me wrong, I can get angry and I do yell at people sometimes. But that's when they don't stick to the game plan we've talked about in the days and weeks building up to a game. When people get out there on the field and decide to do their own thing, I get disappointed and start shouting. But I would never yell at a guy who just made a mistake. We all make mistakes sometimes – I make lots of them – and when one of my teammates does, then my job is not to worry about what he's done, but to simply get in there and save his ass.

Why should I yell at a guy who messed up a clearance or missed a tackle in the buildup to a goal for the opposition? He's disappointed enough in himself already. What he needs at that moment is for someone to come along and give him a lift, not to be told again what he already knows. And it doesn't do me any good to stand there shouting, either. Why waste your energy on stuff that has already happened?

We had a couple of young guys starting in defense that year: Matt Besler, who was only in his second season out of college, and Roger Espinoza, who was also in his early 20s. There's always been a little bit of a coach in me ever since I was a kid drawing pictures of tactics instead of listening to my teachers in class, and I talked to them a lot about different things I saw from my position in goal. But I never consciously set out to be a teacher or assumed I knew more because I had played in Europe. They could teach me things, too, about the way the game was played in this country.

I like to think I settled in pretty quickly, but the one thing I definitely wasn't ready for was the heat as we got into summer. In the hottest months in Denmark, the temperature rarely goes much above 85 degrees. In Kansas City, it was over 100. Playing soccer in temperatures like that is brutal. Even the players who grew up here find it hard, but it was unbearable for someone like me. Just walking to the car made me sweat worse than the old mailman hauling our letters up the stairs in Aalborg.

The only thing that keeps me alive on the field in that kind of heat is watching the outfield players and knowing how much worse it must be for them. I can hardly start moaning while I'm standing back there in my goal and not having to run around. I honestly have no idea how they do it, but I remember swearing to myself that I would never complain about the cold again in my life. I'd rather deal with freezing rain than with such ridiculous heat.

At the start of the season our aim was to make the playoffs, but despite that big win over D.C. United, we got off to a pretty bad start. We won our second game, against Colorado, but afterward we only won one of the next twelve. We were playing better again by the end of the season, but we had left it too late. We finished with the ninth-best record in the league, and only the top eight made it into the playoffs.

It was frustrating because we felt like we would have made it if the season had been four games longer. But at the same time, I think the coaches were pleased with the progress we made. There were so many new players on the team compared with the year before, and it was always going to take a while for everybody to get used to each other and start playing as well as we could. The coaches knew that if they could keep our group together, things would keep getting better the next year.

I went and spoke to Peter Vermes a few months before the season ended, telling him I was having a fantastic time and would like to extend my contract past the end of the season. This team and this place had made me excited about my soccer again, and I knew we had a good group of players who could win trophies in the near future.

He told me he was pleased to hear I was so excited about the project, but the team would not do any contract extensions mid-season, so I would have to wait until the end of the year. That was good enough for me, so I got back to focusing on the next game. Sure enough, when the off-season rolled around, he was good to his word and offered me another year-long contract. I signed straight away.

I'm sure there were other highlights worth mentioning from the 2010 season, but to be honest, it went by so fast. Life flies along when you're having a good time, and sometimes I would sit there and wish I had a pause button so that I could stop everything for a second, step back, and really savor the moment. I have felt like that a lot since we arrived in Kansas City, but that just tells you how much fun I'm having. And this, as they say, was only the beginning.

Kansas City is a lot bigger than the town where I grew up, Aalborg, but in a lot of ways it's pretty similar. Both places have lots of big parks and open spaces, and it makes me happy to be able to give my kids that same experience I had of being able to run around and play outside. It's a great city for children.

20
HOME SWEET HOME

The first three months of the 2011 season were the strangest of my professional soccer career. Our team changed its name during the offseason – the Kansas City Wizards became Sporting Kansas City – with the idea of creating a fresh identity to go with our brand new stadium, Sporting Park. The idea of moving into a state-of-the-art, soccer-specific home after a year of playing at a minor league baseball park was very exciting. There was just one problem: When the season began, Sporting Park was still under construction.

Rather than have us carry on playing at the T-Bones' stadium, the league's organizers arranged for us to play our first ten games on the road, allowing Sporting Kansas City to complete work on the new venue in time for our first home game in June. I had never seen a schedule like it. We would be three months into the season before we got to play in front of our own fans.

Being on the road that much would be tough enough in a country like Denmark, where you can make most journeys in an hour or two by bus and the farthest ones take less than sixty minutes by plane. But in the States, we had to fly across the country to places like Seattle and Los Angeles, as well as up into Canada to play Vancouver or Toronto.

I've never had a big problem with the travel aspect, and I've always been lucky that I deal with jet lag very well. But the thing I didn't think about straight away was the impact of playing so many games away from your fans. Because the distances are so much greater in the US, very few can travel to most road games.

That was a big change coming from Denmark. Even when we were on the road with Aalborg or Vejle, there would always be a good number of our fans at every game. When our team scored, there was a reaction, people would start cheering. In America, you might not have anybody pulling for you, and it makes a difference. As a team, you feed off that energy the crowd gives you.

Playing for the first time as Sporting Kansas City, we won our season opener, away to Chivas USA, 3-2. We didn't win again for a very long time. It never felt to me like we were being outplayed, yet we kept losing by the narrowest of margins – 3-2 to Chicago, 1-0 to Columbus and 3-2 again to New York. We tied 3-3 in Vancouver. It felt like we were getting closer every time, but we couldn't quite turn that corner.

I give huge credit to the coaching staff for how they kept us going during that period. Manager Peter Vermes had such a strong belief in his methods, and he kept doing the same things in practice, refusing to let the results knock him off course. He prepared us each week for the next opponent, but he also kept one eye on the bigger picture. He told us, "If we want to be a successful team down the road, this is the approach we need to take."

We had a great team spirit as well. Unlike my first year, when we had all those new players on the roster, this time we had retained the core of the side from the previous season. We all knew each other a little better, and we were all pulling in the same direction. Peter had done a great job of getting together a group of guys who really bought into his project and had a strong enough mentality to survive a few defeats. We believed in him as a coach, and we trusted each other. Instead of falling apart when we lost a few games, we held closer together and supported one another.

I knew it was only a matter of time before we turned things around. That might sound like I'm being wise after the fact, but I even had a conversation with Peter Vermes about it. After one of the last games in that run of road games (I can't remember exactly which one it was.), we were walking off the team bus and back into the team hotel. I said to him, "Coach, I know this is frustrating right now, it is for all of us. But this is going to change. All we need is a few good results to give us some confidence. Better things are just around the corner. I guarantee it."

196

Our first game at Sporting Park was scheduled for June 9, against Chicago, and you could feel the excitement grow as we got closer to that date. The team did a fantastic job of keeping us involved in the stadium-building process by taking us along for regular tours and showing us how everything would be laid out. It was clear to me from the first time I was shown around that it was going to be a beautiful venue, and the closer it got to completion, the better it all looked. The facilities were awesome, and I couldn't wait to get in there.

A little over a week before that first game, though, I got sick. My family had just got a new pet dog, and I was taking it for a walk one morning when I started to cough. I immediately felt a shooting pain go through my head. I'd had a sore throat and a bit of a cold for a day or two already, but nothing serious. This was the first time I'd felt anything like that. It was extremely painful.

You know how I hate to let illness get in the way of my soccer, though, so I went home, took two Advil, drove the kids to school and headed over to practice. That didn't go well. After a few minutes, I felt like I was going to die – my head was absolutely killing me. I'd played through plenty of headaches in the past, but this was different. I felt like my skull was about to explode. I spoke to the coach and told him I had to go inside, but I still didn't go home straight away because I had a press conference to do and was supposed to be training some kids after practice.

I did both of those before driving home. When I got back, I told my wife, "I'm going straight to bed." I went to our room, closed the door and slept for three hours. Somehow, by the time I woke up it had gotten even worse. It was so painful that I started throwing up, and Jannie made me call the doctor. I had been trying to avoid that because I didn't want them to tell me I had to take a few days off.

So I called and told the doctor what was going on. He said, "Are you able to get yourself over to the hospital emergency room?" I asked why, and he told me that he was concerned it could be something very serious.

It was about 8:00 or 9:00 p.m. by then, but I jumped in a cab and went over to the hospital. They got me in with the doctor straight away, and he did a few tests. When he finally came back with the results, the news wasn't good. "You've got meningitis," he said. "This is pretty serious. You might need to stay in the hospital overnight for treatment."

That didn't work for me, because I was supposed to be traveling with the team the next day ahead of our road game against Toronto. I told him as much, saying, "Listen, I have to get home so I can get some sleep ahead of our trip. Why don't you just give me the medicine and I'll take it."

He said, "No. That's absolutely not possible in your condition."

"I don't think you understand. We have a game coming up and I need to play in it. This is my job. So if you don't give me the medicine, I'm just going to walk out of here without it."

"OK, do whatever you want."

So I did. I left the hospital, caught a cab home and went to sleep. The next morning, I quickly regretted my decision. When I woke up, I was in so much pain that I couldn't even move for the first ten minutes. Every time I lifted my head a centimeter off the pillow, I wanted to scream because the pain in my head was so intense. But even then I kept telling myself, *I have to get up. The team is traveling today.*

Finally, Jannie came and sat next to me on the bed. "You are going to the hospital right now to get some treatment," she said. "You have meningitis, and you want to fly to Toronto to play in a damn soccer game? You can die of this illness."

It took her laying it out like that to bring the message home. I called the doctor and apologized. "I'm sorry, I should have stayed last night," I said. "But I really need treatment right now."

The doctor had seen this coming. "Yup, I knew you would call," he said. "I have a bed waiting, and the staff at the hospital is ready for you."

Somehow, Jannie managed to get me to the hospital. Once I was there, they gave me all kinds of drugs, and I don't remember the next two days at all; they passed by without me even noticing. Apparently, I had slept clean through the game. All I know is that I woke up that Sunday and felt OK for the first time. I didn't know what day it was to start off with, so I had to ask the doctor. As soon as he told me, I started trying to get out of bed. Our first game at the new stadium was scheduled for Thursday night, which was now just four days away.

"I've got to get home," I said. "I've got practice tomorrow."

"No, no, no," said the doctor. "You can't be around people right now. You might still be contagious."

"But I'm on medicine! My teammates will be fine. I need to practice or I can't play in the home opener."

It was almost the exact same conversation we'd had a few days earlier, but this time I knew things must be better, because the doctor caved in. He said, "OK, but you cannot shake hands with anyone, you cannot hug anyone, you cannot share bottles with anyone. You go out there, you have an extremely light practice, and then you go home."

So that's what I did. I called up Coach Pascarella and arranged to have a private session away from the rest of the team. After that, I went home and slept all day. The next day I did the exact same thing. On Wednesday, when I came into the team facility, Peter Vermes asked me if I was going to be OK to play the following evening. I said, "Of course I will. That's why I'm here." After that, I had my practice with John, went home and slept all day again.

At last it was the morning of the game. Kickoff wasn't until that evening, so we met up for another light practice session before traveling over to Sporting Park. Going into the stadium was such a thrill. The locker room was incredible – a hundred times better than anything I have ever seen in my career. Every player had an enormous wood-paneled locker with a huge blue leather chair in front of it, with different ports for all your electronics and music players. Then there were hot tubs and cold tubs and everything else that you might want to use before and after the game.

I don't know if anybody in the US imagines that every team has facilities like that in Europe, but I can tell you they definitely don't. At Aalborg, we just had a wooden bench. That's been the same at almost every stadium I've been to, even when I was traveling with the Danish national team or Aalborg in the UEFA Cup. The only other locker room I can think of that was at all exciting was the one we played in for that Champions League qualifier against Dynamo Kiev in Ukraine.

We were supposed to play that game in the Lobanovskyi Stadium, which is their home ground, but at the last minute they moved it to another venue. When we walked into the locker room, there was a huge brown leather armchair in front of each locker – the sort you would have in front of your TV. And they clearly weren't used a lot; when you put your hand on them, a huge cloud of dust came off. We were all laughing and asking whether anybody had been in there in the last fifty years. It was very charming, though. Each chair had a little coffee table next to it, like you were in your front room.

Sporting Park isn't quite like that. Our chairs are leather, too, but they're upright and designed to help you sit with good posture. They want you to be comfortable in that locker room, but most of all they want you to be ready for a game, and everything has been set up with that in mind.

We had been shown the locker room before we went in for that first game against Chicago, so it wasn't like we walked in there and stood around staring. But it was definitely nice to be in that environment, getting ready for a game and feeling like we were home at last. In most stadiums, the away team's locker room is small and a little cramped, and that's all we'd been used to. Now we had space to do whatever we needed to do. The players who wanted to be quiet before the game could find places to do so, and those who wanted to chat could hop in the hot tub or whatever.

There was a little pressure on us too, though. We had failed to win any of the nine games since our season opener, and one of the ways we had coped with that was to keep telling ourselves, "OK, but we have this big run of home games coming up, so that's where we'll make up all these points we're losing." Now there could be no more excuses. We had a brand-new stadium, and we needed to deliver.

It was important for the whole soccer community in Kansas City that we got off on the right foot, too. The team had put so much work into designing a stadium that looked great, was comfortable and was a fun place to come and watch a game, but fans want to see a winning team. We had a real opportunity to grow the sport in the city because we knew people would be curious and come along to see what it was all about. But if we played badly and lost games, that could put them off right away.

From the first moment we stepped out onto the field, those fans were unbelievable. They were so loud, singing and cheering and shouting. We had good fans when we played at the T-Bones' stadium, too, and a big supporters' network called the Cauldron who were always very vocal in getting behind the team, but the set-up at Sporting Park was incomparable. The new stadium had been designed to amplify the fans' cheers. The baseball ball park had no roof, so if the weather was bad, any noise they made would just disappear into the wind.

At Sporting Park, the fans from the Cauldron had taken over the stand behind one goal, which was the noisiest part of the stadium, but the whole place was electric. The team had arranged a fireworks show and a flyover before kickoff to ramp it up even further. It was a beautiful summer night, with clear skies and the temperature just right for playing soccer.

We played well – taking the game to Chicago and creating some good chances. After about 15 minutes, we scored through Graham Zusi, and the stadium went crazy, except the goal got disallowed for an offside. I remember having to make one save toward the end of the first half, but after the break we came out well again, and between the two teams, we were playing the better soccer.

Photo courtesy of Gary Rohman

Hanging out with our CEO Robb Heineman in the amazing locker rooms at Sporting Park. In all my career I've never known a private owner to be so involved in the running of a club. Robb has a great passion for the game and is greatly respected by the players. Plus he's just a great guy to be around.

And then I got sent off. It was the 67th minute, and Chicago played a ball over the top of our defense for the forward, Dominic Oduro, to chase. I thought I could beat him to it, but I mistimed my run and he got there first. Oduro tried to chip the ball over me, and even though I knew I was outside my penalty area, I threw my hand up to block it. It was a clear goal-scoring chance, so the referee had no choice but to show me the red card.

That was the first time in my entire career I had been sent off. I almost didn't know where to go. I was so angry with myself, not for committing the handball — at that point my only other choice was to give up the goal — but for making the initial mistake of rushing out of my area. I showered and got dressed and a part of me was ready to just walk right out of the stadium and go home before the game was even finished. Instead, I managed to calm myself down enough to sit and watch the last few minutes on a TV in the locker room.

It finished 0-0, though we got cheated at the end. Omar Bravo got absolutely killed in the box by a Chicago defender, but the referee never blew his whistle. That's the way it goes sometimes. I hung out in the locker room until everybody came down so I could apologize for putting them in that situation of having to finish the game a man down.

Nobody on the team seemed mad at me, but what really caught me off-guard was how the local media reacted. I was expecting to get destroyed over my mistake, but instead they were all celebrating me like I was some kind of hero. On TV, everybody was talking about how I "sacrificed myself for the team" by taking the red card instead of allowing Oduro to score. After a while I was like, "Yeah, that's a good point. That was my plan all along."

They wouldn't have reacted like that in Denmark. As I've mentioned before, the press there is so negative, always looking for the bad in every story. Even leaving aside this particular incident, I have always found the attitude in America to be the exact opposite. People always want to hear the good story, the uplifting part, even when you might feel like you're going through a bad moment.

That's not just in the media but life in general — I think the newspapers and TV reflect the way people talk to each other. If I have a bad game for Kansas City, everybody I meet will say, "Keep going," or, "Good, we have another game on Saturday, so we'll have the chance to turn things around then." I love that mentality. It gives you the strength to always keep working hard toward your goals.

In the years since that stadium opening, we have held regular autograph sessions at Sporting Park right after a game; the team will set a few players up at a table and fans can line up to get things signed. In Europe you would never do that, because if you lost, then people would only show up to call you names and smash the place up. The first time we had one of those after a loss in Kansas City, I was so embarrassed that I sat there with my head in my hands, saying, "I'm so sorry," but everybody just kept replying that they were thankful to us for hanging out to sign autographs.

It's yet another reason why I felt so at home in this city. And now our soccer team had a place to call home, too.

I got the first red card of my career during the first-ever game at Sporting Park. It was for a handball outside the area, and I knew I was going to get sent off as soon as I committed the foul. I stayed down on the ground for a second afterward, thinking, What the hell have I done here? Thankfully, my teammates held on to tie the game without me.

Sometimes after a home win, I find myself climbing up onto the advertising boards behind the goal to celebrate with the fans.

21
HOUSTON, WE HAVE A PROBLEM

We'd failed to win our opening game at Sporting Park, but the move to the new stadium still proved to be a turning point. Prior to that meeting with Chicago, our record was 1-6-3; over the remaining 23 games we went 12-3-9. We finished top of the Eastern Conference, which was really quite amazing when you think how poorly we started the year. Again, I have to give credit to Peter Vermes and his coaching staff. They never stopped trusting their methods, and once we finally got that little bit of confidence back, we became a very hard team to beat.

That was an eventful year for me personally. I had made one of the greatest saves of my career, the one against Seattle I described back in chapter 4, where I blocked a Mike Fucito shot and then got up to make a kick save from Lamar Neagle.

Fans in the States seemed to be particularly excited by the kick saves, and I guess they are a little unusual. I've never really thought

Sporting Kansas City's fans like to hold a pep rally, and this one was in 2011, down in the Power & Light District. I went down to say hello, and so did an enormous cut-out of my face made by one of the fans. I thought it was very funny. Our fans are very creative with their signs and banners, and that cut-out showed up at most of our home games throughout the year, too.

Photo courtesy of Gary Rohman

205

much about where they come from, but I guess it's something I learned while playing ice hockey as a kid. I played that sport for a few years growing up – I was the goalie, of course. In a tale that might sound a little familiar, I stopped after getting hit in the face with a puck! I still have a little scar above my eye to show for it today.

The other thing people teased me about in the US was the way I stick my tongue out during games. Usually it's when I'm really zoned in, focusing hard on what's happening in front of me, and I honestly don't even notice myself doing it. My parents tell me I've been like that ever since I was a little kid. Whenever I was studying or trying to concentrate on some tactics I was drawing up, that tongue would just sneak out of my mouth. My daughter Isabella does the exact same thing.

Sticking your tongue out is a bit of a hazard when playing soccer, of course, and I always wind up biting it by accident. When I was at Leicester, there was one occasion when I bit so hard I had to go to the hospital and get five stitches on my tongue. As if things weren't bad enough at Leicester already!

At Kansas City, though, there were other things I had to watch out for on the field. In August, we were playing a home game against Portland, when I got hit in the face by a bobblehead doll.

I must be concentrating on something, because that tongue has come sneaking out of my mouth again!

It was early in the game and Graham Zusi had just given us the lead. I was standing outside our penalty area when he scored, and I started walking back to grab a drink of water from the bottle I keep in my goal. As I bent down to grab it, I felt something smash me in the side of the head. For a second, I thought I had walked into the post.

I grabbed my face thinking: *Owwww!* But when I opened my eyes, I could see the post was a good few feet away. Before I could work out what had happened, my head started throbbing all over. I looked down at my gloves and saw they were covered in blood. I had to lie down – not because it hurt – but because my head was spinning and I wasn't sure I could stay standing up.

The trainer ran onto the field and treated me for a few minutes, putting in a few stitches around my eye, exactly like Granny needed when I hit her glasses in the park! I had no intention of coming out of the game, though, so as my head started to feel better, I got back up and carried on. We won 3-1. I played OK, though my eye swelled up and I couldn't really open it toward the end.

After the game, I found out what had hit me. It was a bobblehead doll in the shape of my teammate Omar Bravo. Sporting Kansas City had been giving them out free to every fan that evening, and a couple of guys decided it would be funny to throw them at me. When somebody finally explained what had happened, I assumed it had been an accident, but then the video footage showed it was two different guys. The first fan narrowly missed me, and then his friend decided to have a go as well.

They were both Sporting KC fans, and I know the one who hit me spent the night in jail. It was supposed to go to court, but it all got canceled at the last minute. People do crazy things when they've had a few drinks, and I know better than most what it's like to be a twenty-something kid making poor decisions. It wasn't the end of the world, though it certainly wasn't the sort of thing you expect to happen when you walk out on your home field.

I used to get stuff thrown at me all the time during road games back in Denmark, usually coins, but on one occasion even a dart. It hit me in the middle of my right shoulder and lodged itself there for a few seconds before I reached around to pull it out. But I still think the bobblehead was worse. That thing was seriously heavy. It was like being hit in the face with a rock.

It wasn't the strangest object chucked at me that year, though. Earlier in the season we were playing Columbus away from home, and at a certain point I found myself running to get the ball back from the ball-boy. Suddenly, something hit me on the side of the face – not hard enough to hurt, but it felt like someone had run up and slapped me. I looked down at the ground and saw it was a hot dog.

I could see a guy celebrating with all his buddies a few rows back in the stands, so it was clear where it had come from. The hot dog was still fresh in its wrapper, so I picked it up off the ground, took one bite and threw the rest straight back at him. I don't remember how it tasted, but apparently they were selling them for $1 that night, so you can draw your own conclusions.

It was a fun season, though. I'm sorry for going on about it, but our fans really are incredible (Well, aside from the ones throwing bobble-heads at me.), and hearing them in the stadium every other week was fantastic. The Cauldron set the tone with the enormous banners and flags they brought along and displayed before the game. They led a lot of the chanting, but the whole stadium got behind us and stayed with us to the end, no matter how things were going. It was always such a positive atmosphere.

Between the fans' support and our improving results, we reached the playoffs full of confidence. In the Conference semi-finals, we destroyed Colorado, winning both legs 2-0 to make it a 4-0 aggregate victory. We then had home-field advantage against Houston for the Conference final, which was a one-off game rather than being played over two legs. We had beaten them 3-0 at Sporting Park two months earlier.

This time, things went differently. Right from the start of the game, we had a hard time creating chances. We were pressing and pressing and pressing, but somehow we couldn't break through. Whenever we made a mistake, Houston came flying back at us on the counter. I don't want to take anything away from them, because that was their game plan and it worked, but that's all they were doing: waiting for us to slip up.

Eventually, we did slip up. Early in the second half, Houston won a free-kick just outside our area and away to my left. Adam Moffat found Jermaine Taylor on the far corner of the six-yard box and I had to dive toward the post to block his header. The ball hit my left hip and spun out into the middle of the area, where Houston defender Andre Hainault passed it into the empty goal.

After that, we had no choice but to throw more and more men forward, desperately searching for that tying goal as the time ticked down. Instead, with about three minutes left, they scored again to make it 2-0. Just like that, our season was over.

It's hard for me to express how disappointed I was that night. I have never cried over a game of soccer, but if ever there was a night when I thought I might, this was it. It was so deflating, so upsetting and so painful to blow that opportunity. As I've said before, losing in finals is tough, but the one thing that hurts me even more is losing in semi-finals. OK, this was technically the Conference final, but effectively it was the semi, since the winners went on to play in the MLS Cup final against the champions from the West.

I had a hard time accepting it was over. I understood how the playoff system worked – I'd been watching the NFL for many years, after all – but I'd never experienced it first-hand. It was so cruel and so heartbreaking to reach that point, believing your season still had another week to run, only to have it swept away. It felt so sudden, so brutal, to realize that this was it, there would be no practice next week, no more games to look forward to.

Even now, I have to admit I'm still not really in love with the idea of settling everything through the playoffs. You fight all year to finish top of your division, but then your season can be over in a flash if you mess up one particular game. I'm sure this will sound like sour grapes, but I still believe they should put the two Conferences together and make it one league where everybody plays each other twice – like in Europe – and then the winner is whoever finishes at the top.

To some extent, I even miss the idea of relegation. I understand that it's not practical with the way the league is set up in the US, but the risk of falling out of the division if you don't perform well enough is an incredibly powerful thing. That pressure to get a result when you are in a relegation battle is unlike anything else in soccer. You become totally aware of how much this game means not only to your fellow players, but to everybody associated with the team. You see fans crying and collapsing and praying to God. You think about the staff in the front office and behind the concession stands that will lose their jobs because the team will lose its TV money from being in the top division.

That pressure is brutal – I wouldn't wish it on anyone – but at the same time, having been down there, I do think that it teaches you something. You come away from it stronger not only as a player, but also as a dad, as a husband, as a person. It toughens you up and gives you a sense of perspective in a way that nothing else in this sport can. Don't get me wrong, there is pressure associated with being at the top, too; you are chasing trophies and you know you can't put a foot wrong because you're playing against the best. But it's different, and in my opinion, you need both.

Having said all that, the defeat to Houston was an even greater disappointment for me than the day I got relegated with Vejle. Maybe it was because I didn't see this one coming, or maybe it was because I didn't have the same emotional connection with the fans in Vejle that I had in Kansas City. I'm not even sure I had ever felt this strongly toward Aalborg's supporters – and I grew up as one of them!

As much as I cared about the city of Aalborg and the people there, the fans always made it feel like they expected something in return for their support, like you had to win their approval. In Kansas City, they loved the team unconditionally. As a player, you wanted to repay them for that, not because they demanded it, but because they deserved it.

When I walked off the field at the end of that Houston game, I didn't just feel like I had let myself or the team down – I felt like I had let the city down. It was a long off-season, sitting in front of my TV and watching and re-watching the tape of our defeat, trying to work out what I might do differently to make sure we didn't put ourselves and our fans through that again.

22
PAINTING THE WALL

The 2012 season couldn't have started any better: seven games, seven wins, a new club record and enough to launch us straight to the top of the standings. We used the Houston defeat as motivation, but we were also fortunate to have almost all the same players back together for another year. Everybody had been working so hard in the off-season to stay in top physical condition, which allowed us to use the whole preseason to work on tactics instead of getting fit.

We play a very physically demanding style of soccer under Peter Vermes, and we've always prided ourselves on outworking our opponents. To do that, you need all 11 guys to be on the same wavelength. If one person isn't doing his bit, it all falls apart. But the whole roster showed up with the right mentality that year. By the time the season started, we weren't just physically dominating teams: we were out-passing them and out-thinking them. We played some very attractive soccer.

Before the season, Peter approached me about taking over as captain. The guy who used to do that job, Davy Arnaud, had left in the off-season, and the manager wanted me to replace him. I was honored, and of course I said yes. I'd already been captain at Aalborg and Vejle, so it was something I was used to, even if it still wasn't something I had actively tried to become.

I had to get used to the idea that I was one of the old men on this team. We had a young side now in Kansas City, full of energetic and talented players in their early 20s, and a few of them had already taken to calling me 'Dad.' Oh man, did that make me feel old! A bunch of the guys started to do it – Dom Dwyer, C.J. Sapong, and Kevin Ellis.

I found it funny, but you can't help but realize they're calling you that for a reason. This is who I was now, that old crank in the corner.

Hanging out with those guys in the locker room made me realize I wasn't young anymore; you get to an age where you have different hobbies and different responsibilities. But on the field it was – and still is – a different story. When I'm out there playing soccer, I still feel like that kid running around a field in Aalborg. I remember thinking the experience of getting relegated with Vejle had aged me because it was so exhausting fighting that pressure every day. But playing in such a youthful, energized environment in Kansas City has taken those years right back off.

As captain, I was lucky to work with such a great group. They didn't need me to do much because there were already so many leaders on the team. And unlike at Vejle, we had a great locker room, where everybody liked each other and enjoyed spending time together. That's probably even more important in America, with all the long road trips you have to make.

Eventually, we lost a few games, but we spent the whole season either top of the standings or close to it. We also had a great run in the US Open Cup, beating Orlando City, Colorado and Dayton. That put us through to the semifinals, where we drew a road game against Philadelphia. On paper it didn't look like a great matchup for us; less than a month earlier we had lost 4-0 there in the league.

Personally, I was delighted to go to Philadelphia again. After a big defeat, the thing I want most is an opportunity to make amends. Having the chance to do it against the team that just beat you is perfect. I couldn't say for certain that we would beat Philadelphia this time around, but I knew we would play better than we had in the first meeting.

In the event, we won 2-0, with Jacob Peterson and Graham Zusi scoring the goals. We were through to the final! It would be played at our home stadium, Sporting Park, a month later. Our opponent was Seattle, which was also enjoying a great season.

The final was played on a Wednesday night in August, and you knew straight away this was going to be a memorable evening. A huge storm was passing through Kansas City, and the referee had to delay kickoff because there was lightning overhead. The thunder was so loud that we could hear it from the locker room, and there were huge hailstones crashing down on the roof of the stadium.

Despite it all, the fans refused to budge. The roof at Sporting Park covers the stands but not the field itself, so when the wind is as strong as it was that evening, it doesn't really protect the supporters very well from the elements. They were wet, they were freezing, they were getting hailed on and they probably should have been a bit more worried about the lightning, but they stayed out there in defiance of it all.

About 45 minutes after we were supposed to do our warm-ups, the storm finally calmed down enough for us to get out onto the field. As I stepped out of the tunnel, the first things I saw were three huge, beautiful rainbows arched over the top of the stadium. The next was the Cauldron. As I've said before, they are always the noisiest fans at Sporting Park, and they have their regular spot behind one of the goals.

At Sporting Park, for some reason, we have always done our warm-ups at the far end of the stadium from the Cauldron, but I couldn't resist the urge to run down there and say hello. I could see the stand was absolutely packed. Half the fans had taken their shirts off during the storm and were jumping up and down, twirling those shirts around their heads. They were singing as loud as I'd ever heard them.

The game was extremely hard-fought, with both teams having some great chances, but we got a penalty in the 83rd minute when one of their players committed a handball in the box. Kei Kamara scored the PK. As you can imagine, the place went nuts. But just when we started to think the trophy was ours, Seattle got a tying goal. It was an out-swinging free-kick, which came in from my left, and Zach Scott put a downward header into the corner of the net.

In a split-second we had gone from being on top of the world to needing to peel ourselves back up off the floor. That's a tough thing to do, but I fell back on the same technique I mentioned earlier in the book, the one where I pretend I'm a film director. I cut out that whole disappointing scene and got back to focusing on how I wanted this movie to go.

It finished 1-1 after 90 minutes, and the game went to overtime. That was extremely tense, but there weren't many great chances for either team. Overtime is always stressful, but you have to keep the same mind-set you had for the rest of the game. You can't start to think, *Oh no, if I make a mistake now, we're finished,* because if you do, then I guarantee you will make that mistake. You've got to play the game as it is.

Neither team managed to score in overtime, so the final had to be decided by a shoot-out. I felt pretty good about the idea. I hold the all-time record for most penalty kicks saved in the Danish league, with 13. The player in second place has 10, and he's retired – as have all the other guys in the top ten – so I'm not likely to lose the record any time soon.

I have a few techniques against PKs which I can't share (I don't want to give away all of my secrets!), but there are two big things you have to get right. The first is preparation, which you do by studying film of your opponents and working out their tendencies – finding out how often each player shoots to his right or to his left – so you have some idea of what to expect.

The second part is psychological. When I stand on the line before each penalty, I am absolutely convinced I am going to make the stop. I imagine myself saving the PK five times over as my opponent runs up to take his shot. The other thing I try to do is get inside his head. I want him to think about missing his attempt, just as I am thinking about saving it.

Our goalkeeping coach, John Pascarella, understood that perfectly. As we were waiting for the shoot-out to begin, he walked over and handed me a piece of paper. On the front was a picture of the goal, with little dots showing where each of Seattle's players preferred to shoot. We had studied those tendencies during the days leading up to the game, so this was simply a little crib sheet to remind me.

But on the back, he had also written me a note. All it said was, "Who has the best record against PKs in Danish soccer history?" I barely even looked at the other side. I wanted to trust my instincts. Instead, I stood there for a few moments, looking at John's message and telling myself I was the best and that none of these guys could beat me.

It didn't work. On Seattle's first PK, I dived left and Brad Evans shot to my right. On the second, Marc Burch blasted it into the roof of the net. Seattle's goalkeeper, Michael Gspurning, saved one of our first two penalties in the meantime. I realized I had to change my approach, and fast.

Rather than go back to the crib sheet, I decided to press down on the "Crazy Nielsen" button. As Osvaldo Alonso came up to take Seattle's third attempt, I did everything I could think of to get into his head. I yelled at him, I lifted my shirt up over my chest, and as he began his run-up, I pointed a finger at the right corner of the goal, telling him I knew where he would try to put the ball. He blasted his shot over the crossbar.

Sometimes that's what it takes in a shoot-out. Much like in my gambling days, I had come into this situation with a Plan A, which was to stay calm, position myself on the line and focus on what I was doing. When that didn't work, I had to move on to Plan B. In soccer, even the best-laid plans don't always work out. It's always good to have an alternative up your sleeve.

I was improvising to some extent, but it wasn't the first time I had tried a similar technique. There was one occasion back in Denmark where I was facing a PK, and just when the forward was about to take it, I ran out of my goal and kicked the ball away. I got in trouble with the referee, who showed me a yellow card, but when my opponent finally got round to taking the penalty, he missed. We went on to win by a single goal.

Zusi missed our fourth penalty, so the score was still 2-2 when Christian Tiffert stepped up to take the next one for Seattle. Once again I did everything I could to distract him, pointing and yelling. I never said any bad words, just stupid stuff like, "I know where you're about to shoot, I've been studying you for six weeks." I backed it up this time by making the save, throwing myself down to my left to block his shot.

Paulo Nagamura took our fifth penalty. He fired it to his right and Gspurning made another great save. You could hear this enormous groan go around the stadium, but then the referee started blowing his whistle. He said Gspurning had come off his line too early and the PK would have to be retaken. As a goalie, I felt bad for him because you do that all the time on penalties and usually it doesn't get called, but I can't control the referee's decision. Nagamura buried his second attempt into the bottom corner.

Now we were 3-2 up. Seattle had one penalty left. If Eddie Johnson failed to score, the trophy would be ours.

Even now when I lie in bed at night and close my eyes, I can still feel how the ground shook as Johnson ran up to take his penalty. The whole stadium was screaming for him to miss, and as I stood there in my goal, it felt like the world itself was moving – nothing could stay still. I started running from side to side, pointing my arm out to the right again and telling him I was ready. It worked. He smashed his shot over the bar, just as Alonso had done.

The next few minutes are a blur. I remember all my teammates rushing over and dancing together on the field. I remember seeing fans climbing all over each other in the stands. And I remember lifting the trophy in the middle of the field while fireworks went off all around. That was only the second thing I had won in my whole career, after the Danish title with Aalborg.

Photo courtesy of Gary Rohman

The moment we won the US Open Cup, as Eddie Johnson puts Seattle's last penalty over the crossbar. I could tell that he had missed from almost the second the ball left his boot.

Eventually, we went down into the locker room where we had beer and champagne. A lot of the younger guys headed on for a night out, but 'Dad' here is a little too old for that sort of thing nowadays. I went home to hang out with my family and go to bed. We had a league game coming up on Saturday, so I had to sleep and get ready for practice.

For me personally, this trophy meant even more than the league championship at Aalborg. The two triumphs came at very different times in my career, and perhaps I took things for granted a little bit when I was younger. Back then, I thought it would be the first of many and I would win even bigger trophies for some leading club elsewhere in Europe. Thirteen years later, I understood how hard it was to win things.

More than that, though, this victory was about a team. It was Kansas City's first big trophy since 2004, and it was so important to make that happen, to finally 'paint the wall' again, as they say over

After the Open Cup win, Mille and Isabella joined me on the field to celebrate. They don't really care about soccer that much, but they'll come down to cheer on their dad. Just on the edge of the picture on the right is Rob Thomson, our Vice-President of Communications, who is yet another unbelievably hard-working guy in this organization – as well as a great guy to be around.

here. The whole organization had been transformed in the meantime, and the team didn't even have the same name. We had needed to show our fans that we were going in the right direction, and we did it.

Things didn't get quite as wild in Kansas City that night as they had back at Aalborg – there was no open-top bus parade and I didn't hear any reports of fans hanging off traffic lights. But I'm confident that if... excuse me, *when* we win our league title... and it will happen... the place will get pretty crazy. Even the people who never used to care about soccer are starting to pay attention in this town.

Photo courtesy of Gary Rohman

Here I am "painting the wall" (or in reality sticking some big metal numbers on it) at Sporting Park to show that we are the 2012 US Open Cup champions. My wife Jannie is the handyman in our household, so this was actually one of the first times in my entire life I've ever been up a ladder. All I can say is that it isn't easy standing on one of those in a set of cleats!

23
HISTORY REPEATS ITSELF

We closed out the 2012 regular season almost as strongly as we had started it. Including the Open Cup final, we went unbeaten through our last 14 games. Once again, we finished top of the Eastern Conference, playing even better than we had the previous year. In 2011, we'd just scraped first place with 51 points, but this time we were way out in front on 63.

Houston finished fifth, meaning it would be our opponent for the Conference semifinals. That was perfect. Here was an opportunity to put right everything that went wrong a year earlier. We had let one bad afternoon destroy our entire 2011 season, but now we could set those demons to rest by eliminating Houston straight away.

Sadly, things didn't work out that way. We lost the first leg away to Houston 2-0, in a game where we didn't play very well but could still count ourselves unlucky. They hadn't particularly outplayed us; in fact, I'd say it was a fairly even game, but they took their chances where we didn't. That left us with a lot to do in the return game at Sporting Park, but I still believed we would find a way. The day before the game, I wrote a note on the whiteboard at our practice facility, telling my teammates that I was not ready to go on vacation yet.

You could tell from the way we played that second leg that none of them were ready for vacation yet, either. We were all over Houston; we completely dominated them. I barely touched the ball once all afternoon. In a game like that, where the ball is down the other end of the field a lot, it can be hard to stay focused, so normally I use a technique I call 'the traffic light.'

As long as the ball is in the far third of the field, the light is on red and I can think about whatever I want – grocery shopping, my kids' school reports, whatever. When the ball moves into the middle third of the park, it becomes a yellow light, and I have to start preparing myself and speaking to my defenders to get them organized. When the ball gets into our third of the field, then it's a green light and I need to have full, 100% focus. I find it an effective way of making sure I'm always zoned in at the right moments, because any goalkeeper will tell you it's impossible to stay fully focused for 90 minutes of every single game when you are standing back there all on your own.

This game was different, though. I stood on the edge of my area the whole time, kicking every ball in my mind. That's the most frustrating part of being a goalkeeper: having to stay so far away from the action, unable to help out when your team is chasing a goal. You have the same feelings of excitement and adrenaline as all of your teammates, but unlike them, you can't do anything about it. You just have to stay where you are and try to ignore the fire burning inside of you.

Houston was defending fantastically, but we still created some great chances. The problem was that we just weren't converting them. Finally, midway through the second half, Seth Sinovic scored one. That

Photo courtesy of AP Images

After we got knocked out of the playoffs by Houston in 2012, one of our supporters threw me this scarf. That word, "loyalty," said it all for me. Sporting Kansas City's fans always stick by us, even in defeat, and as a player that means a lot. It makes me want to work even harder, because those fans deserve something to celebrate.

got everyone believing again, and for the next 25 minutes, we threw everything we had at Houston. It wasn't enough. The game finished 1-0 to us, but the aggregate score was 2-1 to them. It was, without doubt, the most disappointed I have ever felt after winning a game of soccer.

The MLS Cup final was scheduled for the 1st of December, and I had been so sure that none of us were getting any vacation time before then. Instead I found myself back at the team facility a few days after the Houston game, clearing out my locker for the off-season along with all my teammates.

But again, this city is great at picking you back up. In the weeks and months after that loss, every time I ran into a fan they all seemed to say the same thing: "We'll get them next year." And you know what? They're right!

As sad as I am about how the season finished, there were some fun moments along the way. I was named MLS Goalkeeper of the Year at the end of 2012. But much more exciting was getting named to the All-Star team. I've never cared that much about individual awards or prestige – this is a team sport, after all – but the All-Star nomination meant I would get to represent the league during the midseason exhibition game against Chelsea.

It was exciting to train for a few days alongside all the best players in MLS. We had David Beckham and Thierry Henry in the team, both of whom turned out to be extremely friendly guys. It was fun to watch them in practice and test myself against them.

Back when I was playing for the Danish U-21 team, I got to play against a lot of guys who went on to become household names. Italy had Andrea Pirlo at that time; England had Michael Owen, and France had Patrick Vieira. But Thierry Henry was always the player who impressed me most. I remember facing the France U-21 in one game and getting destroyed 4-1 because we simply couldn't contain him.

At thirty-five years old, he might have lost a step, but I still think he's unbelievably hard to play against. He's still quick enough, and he's such a calm finisher. He has a great awareness of where the goal is, and he always does the exact same shot, where he opens his body up and tries to curl the ball around you. As a goalkeeper, you know what's coming but you still can't stop it. He knows how to put just enough weight on it so that you have to dive early to have any chance of getting there. But if you do that, he'll just wait and flick the ball over you once you're already on the floor, making you look stupid. I'm not saying it's unstoppable, but you need to have one of your better days to deal with it... and hope he's having one of his worst days.

We had a lot of fun at the All-Star game, and I was impressed at how quickly a group of eighteen guys from different teams was able to come together. Chelsea fielded a strong side, with John Terry, Frank Lampard and Ashley Cole all starting, and we still beat them, 3-2. The winning goal was scored by Seattle's Eddie Johnson, the guy who wound up missing that last penalty against me in the Open Cup final a couple of weeks later.

The All-Star game is in Kansas City this year, so I hope I get called up again. Who wouldn't want to play an extra game at our incredible stadium, in front of the best fans in America?

This photo is from the MLS All-Star game in 2012. That's me in the back row, obviously, standing next to David Beckham. We had a fun few days together, and best of all we beat Chelsea at the end of the game.

24
LOOKING AHEAD

Many things have caught me-off guard in the three years since I arrived in Kansas City. The warmth and kindness of the people in this town, the quality of the soccer, and the enthusiasm for the game among our fans all came as a wonderful surprise. But the thing I really wasn't ready for was quite how much I would feel at home here. I feel like I belong in this city in a way that I never expected to find anywhere outside Aalborg.

My family tells me they all feel the same. Well, Jannie and Mille do anyway; Isabella is too young to really remember anywhere else. Earlier this year, I was with her for a service at her school chapel, and it finished with everybody singing the national anthem. As we stood, I noticed Isabella was holding her hand over her heart. I whispered to her, "What are you doing?" and she said, "This is how we do it, Dad." I thought, *oh wow! My little girl is already more American than she is Danish.*

That's OK with me. To be honest, if Denmark ever played the US at soccer now, even I might have a hard time knowing who to root for. I'd like to think some of my Sporting KC teammates would be out there representing the States, and if guys like Matt Besler and Graham Zusi were on the field, then I'd probably be cheering for them most of all.

I'm not giving up my roots, though. With technology the way it is nowadays, I feel closer to Denmark here than I ever did when I was playing for Millwall. I know that sounds ridiculous – it's 4,500 miles from Aalborg to Kansas City, compared to just 500 miles between Aalborg and London – but back in the late 1990s, it cost the equivalent of $3 a minute to phone home from Millwall. Now I can call Denmark for 20 cents a minute or speak to relatives for free on

Skype and FaceTime. And you see what everyone's doing on Facebook and Twitter.

Of course, some things are still difficult. Because my father won't fly, he's never been able to come and watch me play for Kansas City, which is a shame because I know he would love to do that. Still, at least there are ways for him to watch the games on TV or via the internet. Again, that wasn't true when I was growing up. I had to make sure I was in front of the TV at the exact right moment if I wanted to see the one English soccer game on TV each week.

I hope my being here in the US will make a few people in Denmark pay more attention to Major League Soccer, and maybe even get some younger players to think about America as a place they can come to develop and further their career. This league is growing, and it's only going to get stronger.

Ten years from today, I believe soccer will be bigger here than baseball. I know people will think that sounds crazy, but I've seen the way the sport has grown in the three years since I arrived. When you drive around Kansas City, you see nothing but parks full of kids playing soccer. There are still kids playing baseball, but they're the minority. I am extremely confident about the future of soccer in America, and the biggest reason is because I see how many young people are taking up the sport.

I like to drop in on those games in the park sometimes. If I'm ever driving by a field and see a big group of guys playing – kids or adults – then, if I have time, I quite often find myself pulling over to join in or offer some coaching tips. It's another way in which this city has reminded me how much I love soccer. Nothing makes me happier than being out in a park and kicking a ball around with twenty random people I've never met. It's hard for me to believe that I was thinking of giving up this sport just three years ago at Vejle.

Sooner or later, I will get too old to carry on playing professionally. We're not quite there yet – I have another year left on my contract with Sporting KC and, the way I feel today, I could see myself carrying on for another three or four years. It helps that there's such a great group of guys in the locker room. It makes me feel young to go in there and have so much fun together every day. They aren't as good at the pranks as the guys at Aalborg, though, and I might have to teach them a few before I quit. Peter Vermes better start being careful with his underwear!

Soccer is a business as well as a sport, so it's up to me to convince the team that I'm still good enough to succeed. At this age, I have to play with the mind-set that every year could be my last. Seeing as I want to win the MLS Cup before I retire, I better get on and do it soon.

After that, who knows? I would love to try coaching, and if there were an opportunity for me to do so in Kansas City, that would be amazing. I always try to stay open-minded about the future, and it may be that an opportunity comes up somewhere else that is too good to turn down. But I would love to stay in this town when I'm done playing. I really would.

Whatever happens next, I'm sure it will be great as long as I have my awesome family with me. I am extremely proud of my little girls, both of whom work much harder in school than I ever did. It would be extremely tough for them not to, of course, because I know all the tricks. I was the world champion of playing hooky, so they would need to be very clever to come up with something I hadn't done before! So far, they haven't tried.

It makes me extremely happy to see how well they've both settled. After the way things went at Leicester, it would have been easy for Mille to get scared about the idea of moving to another new country, but she took it all in her stride. I suppose I better thank Otto the gerbil for helping out, too.

The person who deserves the most credit, though, is Jannie. I've already mentioned all the traveling that comes with playing soccer in this country, with road games that are played thousands of miles and several time zones away. The reason I'm able to make those trips and focus 100% on my soccer is because I know she's at home taking care of everything else. She is the most hard-working person in the world. She's not only a fantastic mother, she's the practical handyman in our relationship, who puts up pictures, repairs holes in the wall, fixes the car and does just about everything else.

On top of all that, Jannie is loyal, kind, and beautiful. I could not imagine a better person to spend my life with, and I'm looking forward to growing old with her. With any luck, that will be right here in Kansas City.

"Welcome to the Blue Hell" reads the famous banner hanging in the Cauldron at Sporting Park. To me, it feels more like heaven.

The sign above the Cauldron says it all: "Welcome to the Blue Hell." Our fans make Sporting Park hell for our opponents, and they are a big reason why we have been able to post such a good home record over the last couple of years. That sign is one of the coolest I've ever seen at a soccer stadium, and it was clearly the inspiration for the title of this book.

AFTERWORD

THE MANAGER
Peter Vermes, SPORTING KANSAS CITY

Selecting Jimmy to be our captain in 2012 was a pinnacle moment for me. The previous captain, Davy Arnaud, had been with Kansas City since my last year playing for the club, in 2002. He had a great work ethic, had been with the team since the beginning of his professional career, related well with the fans, and the players all respected him. He was a hard person to replace.

It wasn't an easy decision to go with a foreign player as captain, let alone a goalkeeper. Not that I had anything against foreigners – my parents are foreigners who came to the US in 1956 – but this is a professional league in America, where we're trying to grow the sport, and I think there are more than enough American players capable of handling the position. So as a rule, I felt the captain should be an American player.

Then there's the goalkeeper aspect. If your team is attacking, and the ball is up the far end of the field, then the goalie is a long way removed from the game. Nothing he says can be easily communicated to his teammates. It's not ideal.

But when I looked through the team and assessed who had the best qualities for the job, Jimmy just kept popping out at me. I didn't make the decision right away, because I was struggling to get over those two hurdles of him being foreign and a goalkeeper, but by the end of the 2012 preseason, it had become so obvious. It was like walking down the streets in China and seeing a guy who is seven feet tall. It pops out because everybody else is the same size.

227

Right from the day he got here, Jimmy had a coach's approach to the game. If an opponent had a shot and it went out of bounds for a goal-kick, Jimmy would go over to the defender while he had a second, put his arm around the guy and say, "Hey, maybe you could do this next time." He talked to them rather than trying to embarrass them in front of 20,000 people. That was a huge benefit to him and the team.

As highly as I rate Jimmy as a goalkeeper, I think he's been an even better leader for the team. All the guys respect him, he doesn't shy away from difficult situations, and he's a real connector of people. Instead of excluding guys, he brings everybody together and makes sure they all feel involved in the group.

When I first announced Jimmy's captaincy, he organized a team meeting. I was only there for the start, but I know they created a little bit of a government within the team. They have a travel minister, a financial minister, an entertainment minister and a few others. He gave all those guys responsibilities for different areas, making sure everybody felt included. I liked the way he took charge and made it happen.

My only concern about Jimmy is the amount of money he seems to like spending on animals. He's told you about the gerbil, but not about the dog he bought after coming to Kansas City. He and his wife went to a charity event and saw this little Labrador puppy which Jimmy took a liking to. They didn't have a dog yet, so he asked his wife, "What do you think?" She wasn't sure, but he said, "Well, maybe I'll just bid on it and see where it goes."

Next thing you know, the bidding is up to six or seven thousand dollars and Jimmy's still going. He had to have that dog. There was somebody bidding hard against him, but in the end that guy had to back down. I like that story because it fits into Jimmy's outlandish character, but it also tells you something about him – he likes winning, and he's a sentimental guy – because really he was getting the puppy for his kids.

He also interacts with the community in a really positive way. In 2012, one lady wrote to the editor of the *Kansas City Star* because she was so impressed with something Jimmy had done. He was just stopping his car one day to get some coffee and he saw some kids playing soccer outside, so he went over to give them a few pointers. One kid's dad was there and was getting worried about this older guy talking to his boy. Then, he got closer and realized who it was. The dad was a big Sporting KC fan, and he was blown away. His wife wrote to the paper when she heard about it.

Jimmy is awesome in those environments. He's so gracious with fans after the game. Certain people do that because it's part of the job, but it comes naturally for Jimmy. I've never come across a person who has said one bad thing about him.

There are certain qualities that you look for in a player. You ask, "Can he play the game? Does he have a good character? Is he personable? Is he marketable?" To get a full package like you get from Jimmy is rare. It's a benefit on all levels to the club, the organization, the community, the city and the team to have a guy like that on your roster.

THE TEAMMATE
Matt Besler, SPORTING KANSAS CITY DEFENDER

The first game Jimmy and I played together was a disaster. He arrived in the middle of preseason, just a few days before we were scheduled to play an exhibition against a team from near our training base in Arizona. The goalkeepers do their own thing a lot of the time in practice, so I hadn't had much of a chance to talk to him before the game, and that always made things difficult. Communication with your goalie is important for a central defender like me.

About 20 minutes before kickoff, it started to rain very heavily. It was like a monsoon, and down in Arizona they aren't used to getting that much rain. The field was really hard and didn't drain well at all, so by the time we ran out to start the game, there was an inch of water sitting on top of the grass. It was like running around on an ice skating rink.

I was slipping all over the place for the whole first half, and guys from the opposing team kept running past me and getting shots off. Maybe there was some nervousness, as well; it was my first game with Jimmy, and we both wanted to get off on the right note. It just felt like nothing was going right.

Jimmy was having a hard time with the rain, too. The ball was so wet that it became impossible to catch, and everything was sliding out of his hands. At a certain point, a cross came in from one of their midfielders and I wanted Jimmy to take it. I was yelling, "Keeper! Keeper! Keeper!" to let him know I thought it should be his ball. He listened and went up to get it, but the ball went straight through his hands because it was so wet. The whole game went like that, just one big mess.

Thankfully, we were able to put that game behind us. Actually we hit it off very quickly. I found Jimmy to be a very refreshing character and unlike anyone I knew here in America. He has a different outlook, and it was fun to see him adapting to life over here. I'm from Kansas City, and it's a place I'm very proud of, so right from the beginning I was giving him advice on schools for his girls, neighborhoods to live in, and anything else that might be helpful to somebody new in our city.

Jimmy and I fell into this tradition where we always wound up sitting together in the locker room after games, just hanging out and chatting. I would give him advice about life in this country, and he would tell me how soccer was played differently in Europe or about the crazy coach who used to hate him when he played in England. I could listen to Jimmy's stories all day.

I was only in my second year as a pro when Jimmy arrived, and he's taught me some really useful things about how to approach the game. One thing in particular that I've taken from him is an awareness that you have to play the percentages. Before he arrived, I had it in my head that I had to block every shot and stop every play. At this level, that's impossible to do. I don't care if you're the best defender in the world, sometimes the forward is going to make a great play or the ball will bounce the wrong way.

Jimmy has helped me to trust in him – and any other goalie I might work with – by pointing out that if I can just make the shot difficult for the forward, rather than preventing it altogether, then most of the time he's going to make the save. We operate more like a team. If I can win the ball, that's great, but if not, I have other options. If a guy's got me straight-up, and he's right-footed, I try to force him onto his left. Or if a forward almost has me beat inside the area, I try to get a little bit of my body onto the guy to keep him off-balance when he's trying to make the shot, rather than sliding in and risking a PK.

That's one of the reasons Jimmy is great to have on your team: he takes the time to talk. With a typical goalie, if you make a mistake and let a forward get a shot off, they'll start yelling at you not to let it happen again. Jimmy is much more positive; he tries to reinforce the good stuff rather than focusing on the bad. I benefited from that a lot. It's probably my favorite thing about him.

THE FAN
Sean Dane, KANSAS CITY CAULDRON

We've been very lucky with the goalkeepers who have played for this team. From Tony Meola through Kevin Hartman and now Jimmy, we've had guys who are not only great at their job, they're also very engaging with the fans. Maybe that's a natural thing, because the keeper is the one player who stands 10 feet away from the fans at each end of the field for a full 45 minutes in every game. But it's also down to their personalities.

Nobody in the US watches a lot of Danish league soccer, so as soon as the club announced it was signing Jimmy, everybody had to go on-line and do their research. We worked out pretty quickly that Jimmy was a world-class goalie, but did we expect him to walk in and be as open as Kevin or Tony? No. He's surprised us all on that front.

One of the great things I see about our league, still in its relative infancy at seventeen-years-old, is that because the salaries are still modest, players are generally more accessible to supporters. When you get guys coming from abroad, they're often taken aback, because you don't see players in the big European leagues going over and talking to the fans after a game. They go out there, play the game, and then they're gone.

But Jimmy just jumped right in, engaging with the fan base from day one. I find him to be an incredibly sincere person. I never feel like he's big-timing you. He's a gentleman who's played at the highest levels in the world and is still more than willing to just talk. He's really interested in what you have to say as a fan, and you don't find that very often in players of any sport.

He also buys us beer. Kevin was actually the first goalie to do that for the fans here in Kansas City, donating a keg to the Cauldron for one particular tailgate, and Jimmy has happily carried on the tradition. I don't know if he was even aware that it existed beforehand, and certainly nobody asked him to buy us anything.

It started in 2011, before our road game against Chicago. A friend, Andy Edwards, was out watching practice, and Jimmy came over to talk to him. He said, "I hear you're going to have people traveling to the Chicago game." Andy told him that it was going to be about 300 of us. He was blown away, and frankly, so were we, because we had never before taken more than about 50.

Jimmy said, "I want to get you guys some beer," and we have never been ones to refuse free beer. So he told Andy to come back the following day, and when he did, there were 300 beers waiting, one for every person. We packed them all into my car, and on the day of the game we loaded them onto our bus, ready for the tailgate. We dubbed them 'Puma Pints,' after Jimmy's nickname: The White Puma.

Last year he did the same again, though this time we had even more fans traveling to the game. He went by the store on the way to practice and loaded up his car with as many as it could hold. Those little gestures go a long way to cementing his place in supporter lore. We even had coasters made with "Home of the Puma Pints" printed on them.

It's not just about the free booze, though. Jimmy shows up to supporter events, sometimes without even telling us he's coming. We organize groups every now and then to go see the Missouri Comets in the Major Indoor Soccer League, and we were there watching a game last year when he just appeared next to me. He came and sat with us and wanted to hang out. Of course, he got mobbed when people realized he was there.

Another time, Jimmy's glove manufacturer approached me and asked if the Cauldron would be interested in designing a special edition glove for Jimmy to wear in a game. At first I wasn't sure – what do I know about glove design? – but we ended up creating something that basically said: "The Cauldron will always have your back" across the wrist strap.

When the manufacturer first put the idea to me, they suggested Jimmy could sign a few pairs at a fundraising event as well, but I wasn't clear if they had spoken to him about it. So I went to check with him and straight away he said, "Absolutely. No problem, I would do that in a heartbeat." I found it fascinating and impressive how he was so ready to both take an opportunity to help out his glove manufacturer – which is a young company trying to grow – but also just spend time interacting personally with the fans themselves.

Of course, he's also a great keeper. It took me a long time to get used to the foot-save. That's a very unusual way for a goalie to play, and to see that the first few times was a little unsettling after watching more traditional keepers for so long. But when you see what Jimmy's been able to do over the last three seasons – not just the double- and triple-saves that everybody sees, but the effort he's put in across the board to becoming the best in the league – it really is commendable.

He wears his emotions on his sleeve when he plays, too, which is something that we as fans identify with. You can tell from the stands when Jimmy's in a good mood or a bad one. After a win, he'll be up on top of the video board cheering with us. When we lose, you can tell how much it hurts him. At the end of the 2012 playoff game against Houston, seeing him collapse on the field – that was how we all felt.

On top of all that, he loves this city. For many years, the foreign players coming into Major League Soccer were arriving at the end of their careers and just trying to grab another paycheck before they retired. That mentality is changing, to the point where the US can be a destination for guys to come and have a good career. Even so, a lot of players still arrive with the attitude that, "I'm here for a few years, then I'm going back to Europe to live the rest of my life." Jimmy is debating whether he wants to go back to Denmark at all. He and his wife and kids have embraced Kansas City as a place to live, and they are a part of our community. To a guy like me who is from here originally, it means a lot.

That approach helps to explain the level of dedication people have toward him now. This community would be crushed if Jimmy announced he was not going to be here next year. There would be a lot people in tears because we want people like that as part of the organization. Thankfully, I don't get the impression he's going anywhere.

JIMMY'S WIFE
Jannie Nielsen

Jimmy and I celebrated our 11th wedding anniversary in December 2012. I am extremely proud to be his wife, but I can't pretend it's always been easy. As Jimmy explains in this book, his gambling continued to get a lot worse in the first few years after we got married.

Every time he told me he was going to quit, I believed him, because it always felt like we had such a great relationship when he wasn't placing bets. Everything was perfect when we were together, but when he was gambling, he forgot that anything else even existed. He would miss family birthdays, parties, everything, because he lost track of time.

But I always believed that if we worked together he could get out of it, whereas if I left, he would have no chance; there would be no reason to stop. What do you do in that situation? He was still the big love of my life, the one that I recognized as soon as I first saw him at the age of thirteen.

The night I found out he was partly to blame for the bookie shutting down, I was disappointed; but I wasn't angry. I'd told him the day before that I could feel something wasn't right; I could read him a little better than he thought I could. Jimmy went out and came back with this big bouquet of flowers, telling me it was nothing to worry about. He said, "It's not a big deal. I can handle it."

It didn't shock me to find out he was lying, because I had already worked out that it came with him being a gambler. I'm not saying you get used to it, but I wasn't surprised. I was just sad because it felt like he was throwing away everything we had together. I did think about leaving Jimmy after that, very often, to be honest. But every time, I always came back to the same question: "Then what?" He was the one for me; there was nobody else out there like Jimmy.

Even I had a limit, though. After the trip to Spain, where he went gambling again with my bank card, I had reached mine. That was when I went to see Lynge. Before we walked into his office, my mom said to me, "I know you love Jimmy. If you think he's worth fighting for, then we'll do it. If you want to leave, I totally understand, and I'll help you to pack."

Thankfully, that was the turning point. Jimmy started going to see Bjorn right after that meeting and gradually got over his addiction. I'm sure some people will think I was naïve for hanging around long enough to reach that point, but they haven't walked in my shoes. Someone like Jimmy doesn't come along every day, and I believe other people see that now, too.

What do I love about Jimmy? Oh boy, do you have all day? I love that he's this big macho guy when you see him out playing soccer, but when he's at home, he's the complete opposite: just a big teddy bear. He's never once raised his voice to me, never. He's always so calm, always keeps things balanced in his head. Not always on the soccer field – I guess he does lose it there sometimes. But maybe that's what allows him to be how he is off the field. He gets it all out playing soccer, then he comes home and he's completely relaxed.

It's so funny how we run this household, because it's not like everybody else's. It's more like I'm the man and Jimmy's the wife. Just yesterday, I fixed a hole in the wall. Every time we go somewhere, I'm the one packing up the car and he's the one checking that the girls have their jackets on. When we're at home, I'm the one hanging pictures while he does the vacuuming. That suits me just fine.

And he's a great dad. He drops the girls off at school every day, he picks them up and takes them to do fun activities. You already know what lengths he went to getting Mille's gerbil over to America so that she would be happy moving here.

I didn't need any extra persuasion to come to Kansas City. I like new adventures, and I've always told Jimmy that I would follow him anywhere. When you move to new places, you always wind up spending a lot of time together because you don't know anybody yet. I've never been sad to spend more time in Jimmy's company.

Kansas City turned out to be better than we could ever have imagined. We love it here, and even our kids are excited about going to school in the morning. I hope we never leave. I would go through all those tough times again to be where Jimmy and I are today.

ACKNOWLEDGEMENTS

This is my second autobiography; the first, *1000 På Rød* (which translates to: *1000 On Red*), was published in Denmark in 2006, but I didn't want this book to simply be a translation of that text. My life has changed a lot in the seven years since that book was published and especially in the last three since I moved to Kansas City. I wanted to write this book specifically for fans of Sporting KC so they could know a little bit more about my story and understand how much their support has meant to me, personally and professionally. Kansas City, you are awesome. Thank you for welcoming me and my family in the way that you have. I hope after reading this book, you will understand how much your support has meant.

The same goes for everybody at Sporting KC. I want to thank Peter Vermes and John Pascarella for giving me back my motivation, my teammates for making it fun to come to training every single day, and Robb Heineman – along with all the other team owners – for risking their money on that crazy Danish goalie that started a fight with a teammate in practice. Hopefully, they don't regret it! Rob Thomson, from our communications department, was also a huge help in getting this book made.

There are so many others I need to thank for their help in getting me to where I am today. Kit Carson for inviting me to play with Norwich as a teenager; Kaj Paulsen, my first-ever goalkeeping coach, for believing in me when others at Aalborg didn't, and Harbo Larsen for teaching me what it meant to be a professional goalie. I had too much help from too many good people at Aalborg to thank them all here, but if you are reading, then hopefully you will know who you are. The whole soccer club deserves my gratitude for always treating me with fairness and respect.

The one person I will single out is Lynge Jakobsen, Aalborg's general manager and my second father. He stuck with me through the darkest moments, always ready to listen and help where he could. I will always be grateful for his support. I know that as I write this he is preparing to move into a well-deserved retirement. Lynge, I wish you only the best for everything that comes next.

For making this book happen, I thank the publisher, Bob Snodgrass, and our coordinator, Beth Brown, as well as everybody else who worked on the project. Thank you for giving me the opportunity to share my story with so many people.

Lastly, I want to thank my family for their love and support, not only through the process of making this book but all the many years up to this point. I was lucky to grow up in a loving home, where both my dad, Ole, and my mom, Bodil, looked out for me and supported me even when I wasn't doing the things I was supposed to, like paying attention in school! I have also always enjoyed great relationships with my brother, Johnny, and sister, Heidi, which is not something everybody can say about their siblings. On top of all that, I had an amazing granny, who took me to the park and played soccer even though she needed crutches to get around. They all helped to make me who I am. My wife's family has also been fantastic to me. Jannie's parents, Mogens and Sonja, are the best in-laws you could possibly imagine.

Then there is Jannie herself. I dragged both of us through hell with my gambling, but instead of walking away, she stood by me and made sure that we rebuilt our lives together, piece by piece. She is the most amazing, strong, kind and beautiful person I know. I look forward to growing old together and watching our two fantastic little girls, Mille and Isabella, grow into young women. Hopefully without making the same mistakes that their father did!

—*Jimmy Nielsen*

The first person I need to thank is Jimmy. It has been a pleasure and a privilege to work with him on this project, and I feel honored to have been a part of it. Throughout our interview sessions, Jimmy's stories left me alternately in stitches and open-mouthed. I only hope that they are as entertaining to read as they were to hear.

A similar thought is due to all the other contributors to this book.

Jimmy's wife, Jannie, was every bit as candid as her husband in discussing how his gambling affected their relationship. Robb Heineman, Peter Vermes, Matt Besler and Sean Dane were also extremely gracious in giving up their time to speak about Jimmy, as were all the other players, coaches and owners who contributed testimonials.

I'd also like to say a huge thank-you to Sporting Kansas City's executive vice-president of communications, Rob Thomson, for putting me in touch with Jimmy in the first place. Both he and the rest of his team at Sporting KC have been an immense help – setting up interviews, sourcing photos and much more. Along with Rob, I thank Molly Dreska and Alice Schroeder for their assistance along the way.

Every book needs a publisher, and I am grateful to everybody at Ascend who helped to make this one happen. Without Bob Snodgrass agreeing to take on the project, Beth Brown coordinating, and Blake Hughes editing, it simply could not have happened. Blake's guidance on differences between British and American usages of the English language was a tremendous help.

Michael MacCambridge, author of several tremendous books on sport, gave me some very sage advice on how to get started with such a project.

Finally, I want to thank my family, and in particular two people. First up is my mother, Rosemary, whose home became my temporary office for the best part of two months as I bunkered down for the writing process. Strange as it was to be back more than a decade after moving out, I feel very lucky to have a parent who would welcome me in as she did.

Then there is my wife, Laura, whose emotional and editorial support could not have been greater. Her feedback on my first drafts was invaluable, as was her patience in dealing with my prolonged absences while working on the book. Her encouragement, advice and love kept me afloat as a tidal wave of deadlines approached. I only hope I can one day return the favor. Principessa, ti amo.

Actually, I do have one more acknowledgement to make. My brother, Alex, did not have a particular contribution to this book, but I failed to credit him properly on a previous piece of work and have felt guilty ever since. And so, belatedly, cheers to Alex as well!

—*Paolo Bandini*

 *Jimmy Nielsen* is the captain of Sporting Kansas City and the 2012 MLS Goalkeeper of the Year. He grew up in Denmark and spent 13 years playing for his hometown team, Aalborg BK – starting a club record 398 consecutive games and helping the club to win its second-ever national championship. During that time he was twice named as Danish Goalkeeper of the Year. After that he had brief spells with Leicester City in England and Vejle in Denmark before joining the Kansas City Wizards – as the team was then known – in 2010. Since then he has twice been named to the MLS All-Star team, and in 2012 he helped Sporting KC win the Lamar Hunt US Open Cup. He lives in Kansas City with his wife and two daughters.

 *Paolo Bandini* is a freelance sports writer and broadcaster specializing in soccer and football. He spent six years on the full-time staff at *The Guardian* – one of Britain's leading national newspapers – before deciding to branch out on his own, and has since worked for a variety of employers including ESPN, The Score, BBC radio and Talksport as well as continuing to write for *The Guardian*. Paolo spent the 2012 NFL season covering the St. Louis Rams for nfluk. com and has since relocated full-time to Missouri, where his wife is studying for her Ph.D. This is Paolo's first complete book, though he previously contributed a chapter about Dennis Bergkamp for *So Paddy Got Up: An Arsenal Anthology*.

Visit www.ascendbooks.com for more great titles
on your favorite teams and athletes.